Experiences with Plants for Young Children

Experiences with Plants for Young Children

by Frank C. Gale and Clarice W. Gale

Pacific Books, Publishers Palo Alto, California

Illustrations by Kelly Solis-Navarro.

International Standard Book Number 0–87015–211–4.
Library of Congress Catalog Card Number 78–88376.
Printed and bound in the United States of America.

PACIFIC BOOKS, PUBLISHERS
P.O. Box 558, Palo Alto, California 94302

To Carl D. Duncan
whose friendship has enriched our lives

Foreword

One of the important factors to be considered when planning a program for very young children is the provision for science experiences. Most two-, three-, four-, and five-year-old children show curiosity about the world around them. What happens when they show this curiosity is important. Their curiosity can be nurtured and stimulated or it may be hindered and stifled. To bring the facts of the world within reach of the child's mind, a program must include a wide variety of first-hand experiences adapted to his interests and level of development. This implies providing each child with a sequence of experiences, rather than subjecting all children to identical experiences. In *Experiences with Plants for Young Children*, Dr. and Mrs. Gale have brought together many suggestions in such a way that a parent as well as a teacher of young children may adapt them to her use.

The pages are filled with ideas to help teachers and parents provide sensory experiences, guide the child's attention to help him explore, compare, and see relationships, and enlarge his understanding of the world in which he lives.

MARY ELLEN DURETT, Professor
Department of Home Economics
San Jose State University
(Consultant, Project Head Start,
Office of Economic Opportunity,
Washington, D.C.)

Preface

The science experiences in this resource book have been planned for teachers and parents to use primarily with four- and five-year-olds; when adapted, they may suggest areas of exploration and direct sensory experiences for two- and three-year-olds. They are suitable also for children of the first- and second-grade levels.

In presenting the materials in this book, it is not the authors' intention to provide a sequential science program for preschool-kindergarten children. Neither is it their purpose to provide all of the many experiences needed in developing any single concept. It is taken for granted that skilled preschool-kindergarten teachers agree that average children seldom develop a concept from a single experience, or even a single lesson.

Rather, in presenting a concept, the book suggests one or more activities as a base from which the teacher can move out, adapting to the special needs of her group, adding other activities, providing environment and materials as her creative ability suggests.

This is exactly what has happened as dozens of teachers in California have tested the materials in this book. Most of them have used the material as the authors intended, not as rigid formulae, but as type experiences, taking care to provide for practice in process skills, in learning basic science information, and in applying these learnings.

It is important, of course, for the teacher or parent to remember that in all the suggested activities, children will benefit in direct proportion to their total involvement. They should participate actively and directly, handling materials at will, feeling them, smelling them, and experimenting creatively and independently in many different ways.

This is a vital part of the learning experience. Once the children are familiar with the materials, the teacher can help them to systematize and synthesize their sensory impressions, guide them in ordering and grouping materials (largely by one characteristic), lead them to the desired learnings, give them practice in the process skills of science—observing, comparing, measuring, etc.—and provide opportunities for them to use their learnings in different situations.

Many more activities have been included than can be used in the time allotted for teaching about plants. It is expected that the teacher will select the concepts and activities most appropriate to her locality, facilities, and the particular season of the year.

The section on Plants and the Seasons is based on the seasons as they usually occur in the northeastern part of the United States. Teachers in the southeastern and southwestern parts of the country will naturally need to follow the seasonal cycle as it occurs in their localities. In California, for example, the seasons follow a wet-dry cycle. Fall conditions and resulting plant changes may not occur until late December or even January; spring growth begins with the onset of late winter rains, which may occur as early as November or December.

Because children in the preschool-primary age groups have a short attention span, the activities should be planned in a context of play rather than in an atmosphere of formal learning.

This is a highly important formative period of life when children gain their first impressions of the world around them, form basic attitudes, and begin to reason and make decisions. The two-year-old and three-year-old learn largely through direct sensory experiences. The four-year-old and five-year-old continue in much the same way but are beginning to be more purposive in their play activities, to ask thoughtful questions, and often to predict outcomes on their own initiative. The older child builds upon the foundations of learning gained during these earlier years.

Broad concepts are developed through accumulated experiences. A child's ideas as to the nature of a root, a seed, a fruit, the sun, a boat, water, etc. are increasingly enlarged as he comes into direct contact with these objects and phenomena and as he begins to solve simple problems involving the physical elements of his world.

The purpose of this book is to help teachers and parents capitalize on the natural curiosity of children about their environment: (1) to give them direct sensory experiences with the objects and phenomena of their surroundings, (2) to build a background of facts and concepts as a foundation for future knowledge, (3) to train them to make accurate observations, (4) to teach them a basic problem-solving skill as they learn to explore, describe, compare, and see relationships, (5) to enlarge their understanding of words, and (6) to provide experiences that will enable them to progress toward such goals as seeing cause-and-effect relationships, making predictions, making measurements, using numbers, understanding simple time and space relationships, and learning to work together.

For the past several years our teaching has included classes for preschool-kindergarten and primary-grade teachers. It has also included work with children of these age levels. Procedures demonstrated in these classes and tested by teachers in their schools and with individual children have shown that the preschool period is not too early for children to begin learning basic subject matter, developing scientific attitudes, and learning problem-solving skills.

Young children *can* learn important facts and develop important concepts. They can learn to observe accurately, examine things carefully, make comparisons and see relationships, make simple predictions, make measurements, use numbers, classify things, solve simple problems, and carry out simple investigations.

An important factor in these learnings, however, is that children must be given the necessary background experiences and that the learning experiences must be presented in proper context and under conditions psychologically and developmentally suited to their level of maturity. If this is done, young children can reason intelligently, carry out simple individual or group investigations, and solve simple problems of their surroundings at a far higher level than is ordinarily expected of them.

The placement of the facts and concepts in naturally topical groupings should make it relatively easy for the teacher to select those desired. The large number of facts and concepts will provide variety from year to year. Two categories of experiences are provided. In one, entitled Exploring, no comparison is involved. The observational powers of the child are sharpened by what he sees, hears, tastes, smells, and feels, for he learns as he explores all that he encounters. In the other, Exploring, Comparing, and Seeing Relationships, the child is asked to make comparisons between two or more objects, events, or ideas—a simple and basic form of problem-solving. Throughout the experiences, he will have ample opportunity to make simple measurements, use properly explained controls in experimenting, count, and note cause-and-effect and simple space and time relationships. Certain concepts and activities have been duplicated in the two categories to group concepts and activities for easier planning.

For their helpfulness in testing the activities in this book, the authors wish to thank the teachers of San Jose, California and nearby communities.

We would appreciate it if teachers and parents who use this book would write to us in care of the publisher, giving their evaluations and suggestions. This would be most helpful in future revisions and enlargements and preparing other books in this series.

FRANK C. GALE
CLARICE W. GALE

Contents

Experiences with Plants for Young Children

1
Introduction

CHILDREN AND SCIENCE: BASIC ASSUMPTIONS

In planning science experiences for preschool and kindergarten, it must be kept in mind that the optimum development of the child is paramount. The focus should be on the individual child—on starting him on his way toward becoming a self-reliant person, capable of developing satisfying relationships with others, directing himself, and solving the many problems he must face in his complex world, first, in the social and physical environment of his home and immediate neighborhood, and later, in the preschool-kindergarten and elsewhere.

From the earliest beginnings of awareness during his prenatal life, through his first experiences of sight, taste, sound, smell, and touch, he has the urge to learn about his world.

In the preschool and kindergarten, the teacher and other adults and children he meets there make up his social environment, and it is in this milieu that he forms interpersonal relationships that will profoundly affect his later life.

The physical environment of the school should be rich in opportunities for the child to wonder, explore, and come to understand the exciting world in which he lives—the world of science. This physical realm is an excellent matrix for guiding his growth and development because he is innately interested in the objects and phenomena of the natural world and is eager to explore them.

Preschool and kindergarten teachers, then, in order to capitalize on this natural urge of children to observe, explore, experiment with, and manipulate things in their environment, should acquire a rich background of science, equip themselves with the necessary materials, and master the proper teaching procedures. Having a sensitive concern for the needs of their children, teachers will plan carefully and guide them in achieving the goals essential for their best development.

One of the goals is the gradual broadening of concepts and the accumulation of an organized body of information from which to reason. In fact, children can develop concepts and acquire information at a far higher level than we expect of them, if the concepts are developed and the information is learned in the proper context. This means linking the familiar with the unfamiliar, the concrete with the abstract, as in the following example.

Let us suppose that the teacher wishes her children to develop an understanding that sound is produced by something that is vibrating rapidly. In children's parlance, the concept can be stated as: "Sound is made when something goes up and down [or back and forth] fast." The wise teacher knows that it is useless for her to strike a tuning fork on the table and tell the children that the sound is made by the rapid up-and-down (or back-and-forth) movement of the tuning fork, because many children will not see that the tuning fork is vibrating. Neither will the teacher ask the children to put their fingers on their throats and make noises as they do so, telling them that the buzzing they feel is caused by their throats going up and down (back and forth), because the children cannot see or realize that their throats are vibrating. What she can do is this: She can place two boards on the table where the children can play with them. Two long nails (or pegs) have been driven into each of the boards and a rubber band stretched between the nails (or pegs). A bead is threaded to the middle of each rubber band and glued there. One rubber band is stretched tightly (Illustration A); the other, somewhat loosely (Illustration B).

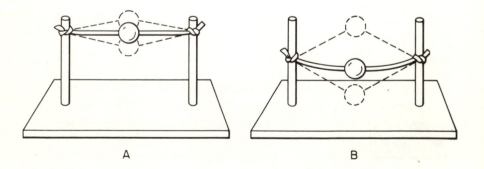

A   B

The teacher allows the children to play with the beads for a time. Then she suggests that they pull up on the loosely strung bead and let it go.

"What is the bead doing?" she asks.

"Going up and down," or "Going back and forth," they will answer.

"Do you hear anything? Any sound?"

"No."

"Let's try pulling up on the other bead and letting go," the teacher suggests.

"Do you hear any sound now?"

"Yes," the child replies.

"How is the way this bead goes up and down [back and forth]," the teacher asks, pointing to the tightly strung bead and then making it vibrate, "different from the way that this one goes up and down [back and forth]?" She points to the loosely strung bead.

"This one goes up and down faster," answers the child, pointing to the tightly strung bead.

"And which one made the sound?"

"The one that goes up and down faster."

"Now can you tell me what things must do to make sound?"

"Go up and down [back and forth] fast," the child answers.

Here is another way of establishing this concept: The teacher places a strip of metal or a thin strip of wood (metal preferred) so that the strip stands out from the edge of the table for at least half its length. See Illustration A.

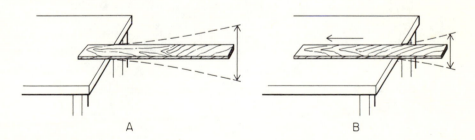

A   B

As the teacher holds the strip, she asks a child to pull the end of the strip down and let it go.

"What is the end of the piece of wood [or metal] doing?" asks the teacher.

"It's going up and down [back and forth]."

"Do you hear much sound?" It is quite possible that if the wood or metal is stiff, it will make a slight sound.

"No."

"Now I will move the strip back on the table," says the teacher. See Illustration B.

Again a child is asked to pull on the strip and let it go.

"Do you hear anything?"

"Yes."

"How is the way the strip went up and down [back and forth] when it made a sound different from the way that the strip went up and down [back and forth] when it did not make a sound?"

"It went up and down [back and forth] faster."

Note that in each case the teacher makes a clear connection between the up-and-down [back-and-forth] visible motion (vibration) of the rubber bands or strips that produce only a little (or no) sound and the much more rapid and more difficult-to-see vibrations that produce definite, louder sound.

A different example can be used to teach the children about air. During the time when the children are playing with objects in a tub of water, a teacher will sometimes stuff a paper napkin in the bottom of a water glass and, inverting it in the water, push it downward. See illustration below.

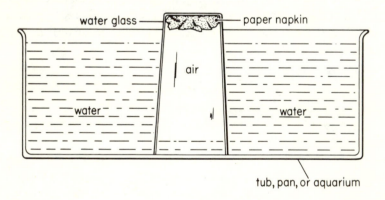

The teacher then lifts out the glass and shows the children that the napkin is still dry, explaining that the water could not come into the glass and wet the paper napkin because there was air in it. In doing this, the teacher robs the children of an opportunity to discover and state this truth for themselves. The concept, "Air takes up room," is a difficult one for young children to understand because air is not visible. It is doubtful that they truly comprehend it, even after being shown the foregoing demonstration and having it explained to them. The concept will be made easier if, in conjunction with the demonstration, the teacher adds the following procedure. She places a large carton on the floor, pins a label AIR on one child and WATER on another, explaining the meaning of the labels to the children. She tells them they are to pretend that the carton is the water glass, that one child is the water, and the other child is the air in the glass. Then she tells the child marked AIR to get into the box. When he crouches down, he fills the carton. Now she asks the child labeled WATER to get into the carton also. He cannot. See illustration.

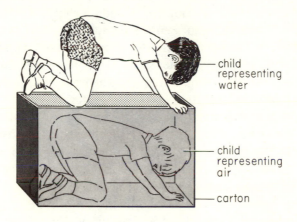

child representing water

child representing air

carton

Be sure that the carton is not too big or both AIR and WATER will be able to get into it.

Now the teacher asks, "Why can't WATER get into the carton?"

"Because AIR takes up all the room," the children answer. The teacher then returns to the original demonstration and repeats it. As she pushes the glass down into the water, she says, "Remember what happened when Billy, who pretended to be the water in this tub, tried to get into the carton, which we pretended was the water glass? And when John, who pretended to be the air, was in the carton? Now can you tell me why the water cannot get into the glass?"

"Because the glass is full of air," the children answer.

In this experience, the children did not exactly express in words the concept that air takes up space, but the idea was clear, and the episode of the children and the carton helped to make the concept of air (an invisible substance) concrete.

THE LEARNING ENVIRONMENT

Young children learn primarily through play, the two- and three-year-olds as individuals or in groups of two or three. The four- and five-year-olds often are brought together in larger groups for special experiences.

For all of them, however, the learning environment should be without pressure—relaxed and informal. The physical arrangement of rooms and playground and the placement of equipment and materials in these areas should be such as to allow the children to move about freely from one activity to another. The selection of materials and equipment should provide for a wide variety of science experiences related to the different centers of activity.

The teacher should plan definite science-related experiences for such centers of activity as the sand box, the water tub, and the teeter-totter in the playground area; for the finger-painting materials, the building blocks, and the playhouse materials in the classroom; as well as for activities associated with excursions and such phenomena as rainy weather, snow, etc. For example, two five-year-olds may be playing in the sand box making mountains and filling cans with sand. The teacher joins them. She has brought with her a watering can full of water and a container filled with fine clay soil. She suggests that it might be fun to make a lake in the sand. One of the children makes a depression in the sand and pours water into it. The water disappears. The teacher then suggests that they pour some of the fine clay soil into the depression and make a new depression in it. When the children pour the water into the clay-lined depression, the water does not seep away. Through this experience, the children have become aware that some soils hold water better than others, whether they express the idea in words or not.

THE ROLE OF THE TEACHER

A well-trained and perceptive teacher is vital to the school program. Without her, the experiences are apt to result in little more than generalized impressions, significant though these may be. Without specific learnings, the experiences lose much of their value. Of course, in any science experience, the teacher can tell the children the answers; but if she does this, she marks herself as a dispenser of information and monitor of materials and destroys the opportunity for the children to make discoveries for themselves, rather than serving as a guide who directs their explorations. The teacher with a rich background in science can help the children to systematize their generalized explorations and to verbalize the facts and concepts involved.

In the following example a group of four- and five-year-olds is gathered around a table on which the teacher has placed a number of magnets of different sizes and shapes, together with a miscellaneous assortment of items—pieces of string and cloth, rubber bands, bits of wood, paper clips, small nails, etc. After the children have played with the materials for a while, the teacher asks, "Are you having fun? What have you found out?" The children show her nails, clips, and other bits of iron and steel clinging to the magnets. One of them may say, "My magnet picks up nails."

"Do your magnets pick up everything on the table?" asks the teacher.

The children experiment some more and find that the magnets pick up some of the items (bits of iron and steel) but not others (rubber bands, bits of cloth, wood, etc.). The teacher places two cardboard boxes on the table and suggests that the children put the things that the magnets pick up into one box and the things the magnets do not pick up into another.

Through adroit questioning and seemingly casual suggestions, the teacher has helped the children to systematize their exploration. Without their realizing it, she has led them to understand that magnets attract some things and do not attract others. She can also lead the more mature children in the group to see that one magnet repels another, though all attract certain things, and that they attract through things (water, cloth, paper, thin strips of wood, etc.). They discover these truths for themselves under conditions of enthusiastic play. Through the whole experience, the teacher has been the unobtrusive guide, knowing what materials are needed, what suggestions to make, and what questions to ask.

The imaginative, well-trained teacher will help the children to make use of their learnings to solve simple problems. For example, the experiences with magnets can be followed up by (1) dropping a small nail or paper clip into a glass of water and asking the children to find ways to get it out without using a spoon or other implement or getting their hands wet; (2) spilling paper clips or bobby pins on the floor and asking them to think of a way to pick them up quickly with-

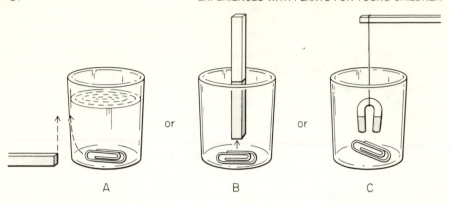

A   B   C

out using only their fingers. She may suggest to the children that they recall what they learned from their play with magnets. See illustration.

As the teacher moves from one child to another or from one group to another, she should be on the lookout for opportunities to help the children to look at things carefully, to describe them accurately, to make comparisons and see relationships, to note cause-and-effect relationships, and to make simple predictions.

Without making preliminary explanations, the teacher can also, wherever the situation presents itself naturally, build the foundation for a later awareness of the value of the use of a *control* and of keeping all elements of the experimental situation *constant* except the variable being tested. For example, the question may be asked, "What do seeds need to sprout?" or "What makes seeds sprout?"

Some child suggests that seeds need water to sprout.

"Shall we see if Sally is right?" asks the teacher.

The children, then, under the teacher's guidance, plant radish seeds in pots, jars, or cut-down milk cartons that have been filled with dry soil. The teacher makes sure that the planted seed containers are placed together in pairs. She gives the children small cups and tells them to fill them with water and to pour the water into one container of each pair, but not into the other. The teacher will need to determine how many cups of water each plant container needs to have the seeds properly watered. See illustration.

If it is necessary to water the seeds again, the children should use the same cups and pour the same amount of water into the containers of each pair that they watered when they first planted the seeds.

In this experience, the *control* was the unwatered pot of seeds. The *constants* were the size of the pots and the amount of soil and

A scientific procedure was followed, though the children were un-
aware of the fact. By bringing elements of scientific procedure into
her children's experiences, the teacher is laying a foundation for a
later awareness of the importance of such items as *controls*, *constants*,
and *variables* and the use of scientific procedure.

YOUNG CHILDREN AND PROBLEM-SOLVING

Experiences that involve observing two or more objects simulta-
neously, comparing them, and seeing the relationships involved are
too advanced for most two- and three-year-olds. For them, experiences in science should consist of a rich variety of sensory experiences
to provide the opportunity for exploration of the child-world, to give
concrete meanings to words, and enjoyment and understanding of
their physical environment and a growing awareness of their relation
to it.

The two-year-old or three-year-old is first asked to run his hand
over a piece of coarse sandpaper while the teacher says over and
over, "Rough! Rough!" Then she tells him to run his hand over a
smooth object and repeats the word, "Smooth! Smooth!" Or she
may let him hold bits of wood or cork in his hand and say, "Light!"
as she shows how to lift them, and then give him lead fishing weights
or pieces of heavy rock and say, "Heavy!" as he lifts them. Or again,
she may say, "Warm!" as the child puts his hand into a container
filled with warm water and "Cold" when he puts his hand into very
cold water.

The four-year-old and five-year-old, however, can be guided to
explore more systematically. For them, problem-solving is a matter
not only of examining things with all of their senses, but also of
describing accurately what they see, hear, smell, taste, or feel, comparing two or more objects or phenomena, seeing relationships between or among them, and drawing conclusions.

The following experience working toward a definition of the concept *fruit* illustrates the foregoing points.[1] (The concept and a de-

---

[1] Robbins and Weier define a fruit as a "mature ovary of a flower with its one or more seeds;
sometimes other parts of a flower or inflorescence may be intimately associated with the mature
ovary." (Wilfred W. Robbins and T. Elliot Weier, *Botany*, John Wiley and Sons, Inc., 1950,
p. 208.)

Wilson and Loomis define a fruit as a "ripened ovary (or group of ovaries) containing the
seeds, together with adjacent parts which may be fused with it at maturity." (Carl L. Wilson
and Walter E. Loomis, *Botany*, The Dryden Press, 1957, p. 508)

In the botanical sense, a pineapple, kernel of corn or grain of wheat, bell pepper, cucumber,
and squash are all fruits.

scription of the procedure are given on page 30 of this book.) The description of the activity and the dialogue are a modification of an actual tape recording of the experience with a group of five-year-olds. In this case, the teacher placed a number of different kinds of fruit on a table.

TEACHER (pointing): Can you tell me what this is?

CHILDREN: A cantaloupe.

TEACHER: A cantaloupe. That's right. Now let's see what else we have here. What is this?

CHILDREN: A lemon.

TEACHER: That's fine. And if that is a lemon, what is this?

CHILDREN: An orange.

TEACHER: And what is this?

CHILDREN: A tomato.

TEACHER: That is correct. Do you know what this is?

CHILDREN: A squash.

TEACHER: Yes, this is a squash. Now can you tell me what this is?

CHILDREN: A peanut.

TEACHER: It is a peanut. Let's open the peanut. Now let's cut each of the other things in half.

The teacher places each fruit on the table with the cut side facing up.

TEACHER: Now I want to ask you something. Look at all of these. Do you see any way in which they are all the same? I'll give you a hint. It is not their size or color.

SUSIE: There's a seed.

TEACHER: Susie says there is a seed inside this one. Will you take a look, Jim, and tell us if she is right? Do you see any seeds?

JIM: Yes, I see a seed. I see lots of seeds.

ANOTHER CHILD: I love seeds.

TEACHER: Come over here, Burton. You take a look too. Do they all have seeds in them?

Burton does not answer—just looks.

TEACHER: You point out the seeds in this one, Carol. Where are the seeds here?

Carol points them out.

The teacher continues in this fashion, having each child take a turn in pointing out the seeds. Finally, she asks Burton to point out one and Burton does so.

TEACHER: That's good, Burton. That's good, children. Now do you know what we call things that have seeds in them?

CHILDREN: What?

TEACHER: We call them fruits. And what do fruits usually have in them?[2]

CHILDREN: Seeds.

TEACHER: When you go home, see if you can find other things in your garden or among the things Mother brings home from the grocery store that are fruits. And how are you going to know they are fruits?

A CHILD: Oh, well, you have to look and see if they have seeds.

SEVERAL CHILDREN: Seeds, seeds.

TEACHER: Yes, they will have seeds inside them. Does an avocado have a seed inside of it?

A CHILD: I guess so.

TEACHER: When you go home, ask your mother to buy an avocado and see if there is a seed inside.

A CHILD: O.K.

TEACHER: That's fine. You children did very well.[3] "When you go home, see if you can find other things in your garden or among the things Mother brings home from the grocery store that are fruits." This follow-up helps to fix the definition in the children's minds and to insure its retention.

---

[2] All wild fruits contain seeds. However, in some cultivated varieties such as navel oranges, seedless grapes, bananas, etc., the seeds have been bred out.

[3] Notice that the teacher developed the concept *fruit* broadly by using not just one or two kinds of fruit, but by using a wide variety of fruits. The children observed, compared and saw one common factor or relationship among the fruits—the seeds. Notice also that the teacher gave the children specific guidance as to what to look for and steered them away from elements that might have confused them. "It is not the size or color." And finally, observe that the teacher made provision for following up the experience to have it repeated in a different context.

2

Differences and Similarities in Plants

EXPLORING

A. Plants are made up of different parts

Stems

Plants have different kinds of stems.

Show different kinds of plant stems—green, woody, etc. Let the children examine them and talk about them.

Some plants send out stems that grow on top of the ground.

Get some strawberry plants that have runners with new plants at the tips. Set these plants in soil in a box. Show other plants with runners—crab grass, violets, etc.

Strawberry plant with runners

Stems of vines climb by clinging to things.

Show vines like English ivy, Boston ivy, Virginia creeper, creeping fig, etc., that send out roots at the joints to use in climbing. Show vines like sweet peas, beans, etc., that climb by twining around other plants.

Stems of vines need to be held up by something.

Plant a bean or some other vine in a box or flower pot with a stake to support it. Remove the stake and show the children how the vine collapses when the supporting stake is taken away.

Buds

Buds grow on branches.

Let the children examine different kinds of winter twigs of deciduous trees. Point out the buds. Take the children for a walk to see trees that have dropped their leaves. Point out the buds. If there is a deciduous (leaf-dropping) tree near the school, have the children follow the changes through the year—leaves, bare branches, branches with buds, opening buds, and development of new leaves.

There is a bud between a leaf stem and the branch it grows on.

Bring in some leafy branches that have distinctly formed buds between the base of the leaf stalk and the stem. Let the children locate and examine the buds. Let them pull

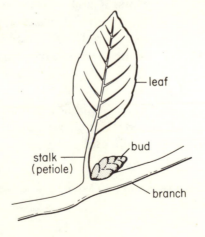

leaf

stalk
(petiole)

bud

branch

off the leaves to see what the branches will look like in winter. Tell them that in warm places like California many trees are evergreen and do not have buds in their axils (the angle between the leaf stalk and the branch).

Leaves

There are different kinds of leaves.

Bring a variety of leaves to class. Let the children examine and describe the different kinds in terms of shape, tips, margins, color, etc. Take them for a walk to observe leaves and have them pick as many different kinds as they can find.

Flowers

There are many different kinds of flowers.

Take the children for a walk to see flowers. Point out the different kinds and talk with them about colors, sizes, shapes, fragrance, etc.

Some plants do not have flowers.

Show the children ferns, mosses, and other plants without flowers. Have them look for flowers and discover there are none. (They should not be kept looking in vain.)

Fruits

There are many different kinds of fruits.[1]

Show the children many different kinds of fruits. Teach them that all *natural* fruits have seeds. (Certain fruits have had their seeds bred out of them—navel oranges, seedless grapes, bananas, pineapples, etc.)

Seeds

There are many different kinds of seeds.

Show the children many different kinds of seeds taken from plants—pumpkin, tomato, peach, etc.

---

[1] The children should have already had the lesson on the distinguishing characteristics of fruits, i.e., fruits have seeds.

Plants have seeds in many different kinds of containers.

Show a variety of ripe fruits that have seeds. Cut them open and let the children find the seeds.

Show plants such as beans and peas that have seeds in pods.
Show cones of coniferous trees (fir, pine, etc.) and their seeds. (If the cones are picked up when they are ripe but unopened, they will usually open up and release their seeds.)

B. There are many different kinds of plants

Most plants grow in the ground.

Show a variety of plants, or pictures of plants, that grow in the ground—trees, shrubs, flowers, mosses, ferns, other non-seed plants, etc. Take the children for a walk to see how many different kinds of trees they can see. Bring in small branches from many different kinds. Take another walk to observe shrubs and flowers or ferns and mosses.

Some kinds of plants live in the ocean.

Take a field trip to the seashore. Before you go, show the children samples of different kinds of seaweed—green, brown, etc. Bring some bits of seaweed back to school. Or show colored pictures of different colored seaweed.

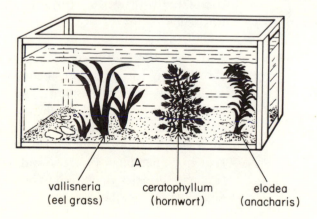

A

vallisneria   ceratophyllum   elodea
(eel grass)   (hornwort)   (anacharis)

Some kinds of plants live in streams and ponds.

Take the children for a trip to a pond or stream. Let them see how many different kinds of plants they can find along the banks of the pond or stream. Collect and show different kinds of plants that grow in the water of streams and ponds. Plants common to this situation would be cattails, tule, duck weed, arrowroot, water fern, water hyacinth, and various kinds of rushes.

Some kinds of plants grow under water.

Set up an aquarium and stock it with a variety of algae and other underwater plants. (These plants may be secured at a pet shop.) Take the children for a walk to a stream or pond and show them the different kinds of plants that are growing under water.

Some kinds of plants do not have seeds.

Show different kinds of living fungi, mosses, and ferns. Have the children look for seeds and discover there are none. Then tell them that these kinds of plants do not have seeds, but grow spores. Cut off the cap of a mushroom, place its gills down on a piece of dark paper over night. In the morning, the paper will be covered with lines of spores. Show the children the brown spore cases (sori) on the under side of a fern frond. Tell them that these brown cases are full of spores and that ferns and mosses grow from spores, not seeds.

There are different kinds of ferns, mosses, liverworts, and lichens.

Show pictures of different kinds of ferns or show living or pressed specimens. Show samples of mosses, liverworts, and lichens, either living or pressed, or show pictures of them, in color, if possible. Take the children for a walk and point out to them the lichens growing on trunks of trees and on rocks. (Lichens consist of a fungus and a green algae living together.)

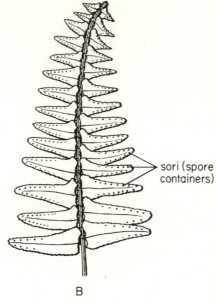

sori (spore
containers)

B

Fern leaf (frond)

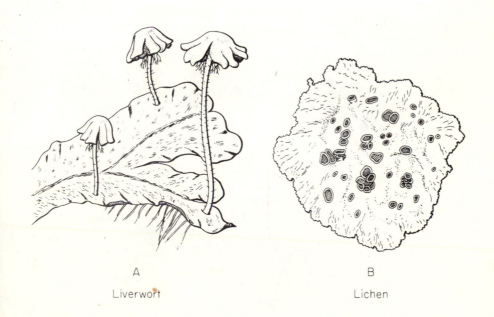

A

Liverwort

B

Lichen

C. Plants grow to be different sizes

Some plants are very big.

If possible, take the children to a large grove of trees. (In California, a trip to the giant redwoods would be most rewarding.) Show them tiny seedlings and tell them how long it takes for these trees to grow so large. Sometimes large trees grow in or near the schoolyard.

Point out many different plants and discuss their sizes with the children. The school yard will usually provide a sufficient number of examples.

Some plants are so small that we must use a microscope to see them.

Secure a microscope (one with two eye-pieces) and explain its use to the children. Place a drop of yeast culture on a slide. Adjust to high power. Let the children look through the microscope. Now have them look at the culture slide with the naked eye. All they will see will be a milky smear. If some of the children have difficulty seeing anything through the microscope, draw a picture of several yeast plants and show

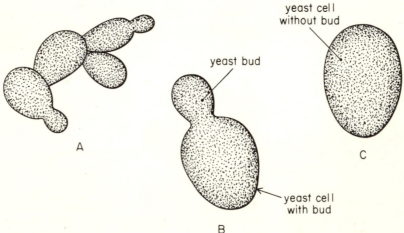

A

yeast bud

yeast cell
without bud

yeast cell
with bud

B

C

them to the children. (A culture of yeast may be made easily by adding part of a yeast cake to a cup of warm water in which two teaspoons of sugar have been dissolved. Place the mixture in a warm place.)

Bring in some green pond or aquarium water. Tell the children that the green water has many tiny plants and animals in it, but they are so small that they cannot be seen without a microscope. Then place a drop of water on a slide, together with some green scum or algae, and let the children look through the microscope.

EXPLORING, COMPARING, AND SEEING RELATIONSHIPS

A. Plants are made up of different parts

Roots

Not all roots look the same.

Question: Do all roots look the same? Show a variety of roots. Have the children compare them as to shape, size, etc.

Some plants have one main large root (tap) with small roots coming out of it; other plants do not have one main (tap) root. Instead they have many smaller roots.

Question: What are the two main kinds of roots? See if the children can put the roots into the two groups—those with one main (tap) root, i.e., carrot, beet, parsnip, and those without one main root (fibrous roots), i.e., grass, corn. If the children have difficulty doing this, place a plant with a tap root (carrot, mallow, filaree, etc.) at one end of a table and a plant with fibrous roots at the other. Let them group the rest of the plants with the two known plants on the basis of the kind of root each has.

Stems

There are different kinds of stems.

Question: Do all stems look alike? Show a variety of stems. Have the children compare them as to color, bark, flexibility, etc.

We can usually know the kinds of trees and other plants by their stems.

Question: Can we sometimes tell what kind of tree it is by looking at the bark on the trunk? Show pieces of bark (or pictures) from different trees. Also show pictures of tree trunks. Take the children for a walk to look at tree bark and tree trunks. Each kind of tree has its own kind and pattern of bark. Tell them that a tree trunk is a stem.

Different kinds of trees have different kinds of bark.

Some trees have one main stem; others have more than one main stem.

Question: What are the two main kinds of tree stems? Show pictures of different kinds of trees. See if the children can put them into two groups—those with one main central stem (most coniferous trees such as fir) with branches coming out from it, and those with more than one main stem (many broadleaf trees such as elm). Take the children for a walk to look at trees. Have them compare the trees as to whether they have one main stem or more than one.

Usually trees have one main stem coming out of the ground; bushes have more than one main stem coming from the ground.

Question: How can we tell a tree from a bush? Take the children for a walk to look at trees and shrubs (bushes). Have them compare the trees with the shrubs as to the number of stems they can see coming from the ground. (A loose distinction is that trees are larger than shrubs.)

Buds

There are different kinds of buds.

Question: Where are buds found on branches of trees? Let the children examine different kinds of winter twigs. Help them to see that some of the buds are on the sides of the twigs (lateral); others are on the tips of the twigs (terminal).

Buds are different in size, shape, and color.

Question: Are all buds the same? Show winter twigs from different plants. Let the children handle and examine them and compare the buds by size, color, and shape.

Leaves

There are two main kinds of leaves.

Question: What are the two main kinds of leaves? Bring to school a variety of simple leaves (those that have a leaf stalk with one leaf blade on it) and compound leaves (those that have a leaf stalk with more than one leaf blade on it). Ask the children to put them into two groups. If they find this too difficult, place a simple leaf at one end of the table and a compound leaf at the other. Help them to understand the way in which they differ.

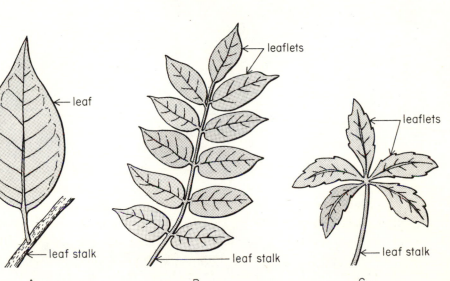

A	B	C
Simple leaf	Pinnately compound leaf	Palmately compound leaf

There are many different kinds of leaves. Different kinds of leaves have different shapes, tips, and edges.

Question: Are all leaves the same? Bring a variety of leaves. Have the children compare them and put them into two piles according to their similarities in shape, size, tips, or margins, etc. Take the children for a walk to collect leaves. Back at the school, have them compare and group the leaves according to similarities. Discuss the similarities and differences with them. (There will have to be several sortings, according to the differing criteria.)

Some plants have wide leaves; others have narrow leaves.

Question: Are all leaves the same width? Bring to school a variety of small branches of coniferous (cone-bearing) and broad-leaf trees. Have the children compare the leaves and put them into two groups—narrow-leaf and broad-leaf.

The kinds of leaves trees and other plants have help us to know them.

Question: Can we tell by looking at leaves what kind of tree or other plant we are looking at? Take the children outside to look at trees and other plants. Get them to compare *all* of the leaves of one kind of tree or plant with *all* the leaves of another kind of tree or plant. Help them to recognize different kinds of plants by their leaves. Name the plants and trees and see how many plant leaves the children can name. Use leaves of orange, lemon, grapefruit, fir, spruce, etc.

A
Pinnate (feather) venation

B
Palmate (hand) venation

Different kinds of plants have different kinds of vein lines in their leaves.

Question: What kinds of veins do leaves have? Bring in a variety of leaves. Have the children compare them as to their veins. Have them put them into two piles—those that have one main vein with smaller veins coming from it (pinnate venation) and those with several main veins (palmate venation).

Flowers

Flowers do not all look the same. There are many different kinds of flowers.

Question: Do all flowers look the same? Show the children many kinds of flowers or brightly colored pictures of flowers. Let them tell how each flower is different from others. Let them examine them, smell their fragrance, and tell about the feel of each one.

Each kind of plant has its own kind of flowers.

Question: Does one kind of plant have different kinds of flowers? Show a variety of annual plants with flowers. Have the children look at all the flowers on each plant. Help them to recognize that each kind of plant has only one kind of flower (its own kind).

The petals of some kinds of flowers are joined.

Question: Are the petals of all flowers separated from each other? Show a variety of flowers, some, like morning glory, phlox, etc., having joined petals. Place a joined-petal flower at one end of the table and a separate-petal flower (rose, buttercup, fruit blossom such as peach or apricot, or a strawberry blossom) at the other. Ask the children to put each of the other flowers in the joined-petal or separate-petal pile. (The children should have learned already what petals are.)

*Flowers have
different sizes,
shapes, and colors
of petals.*

Question: Are the petals of flowers the same? Bring to school a varied collection of flowers. Help the children pull off the petals and stick these to a piece of paper with Scotch tape or paste. Get them to see that the petals are different in size, shape, and color.

*Some flowers grow
in clusters; others
grow alone.*

Question: Is there always just one flower on a stalk? Show different kinds of flowers, some with only one flower to a stalk; others, with more than one.

*Flowers help us
to tell plants apart.*

Question: Can we tell what kind of plant we are looking at by its flowers? Bring to school plants and small branches with flowers. Name the plants. Let the children see how many of the plants they can name by looking at the flowers. (This activity may be used for identifying leaves, fruits, and seeds also.)

Fruits

*There are many
different kinds of
fruits.*

Question: Are there many different kinds of fruits? Show the children many different kinds of fruits and let them compare them as to size, color, shape, fragrance, taste, etc.

*Fruits help us to
tell plants apart.*

*Fruits from the same
tree or plant are all
the same.*

*Each kind of plant
has its own kind
of fruit.*

Question: Can we tell what kind of plant we are looking at by its fruit? Place several fruits of the same kind on the table. Repeat for a variety of kinds of fruit. Have the children compare the fruits from the same kind of plant with those from other plants. Show the children several plants of the same kind, each with mature fruit. Let them compare these with several sets of plants, each with the same kind of plant for a set. Help the children to identify each kind of plant by its fruit.

Fruits usually have seeds inside them.

Question: In what way are nearly all fruits alike? Show the children different kinds of fruits. Cut the fruits open. Try to get the children to tell you that nearly all of the fruits have seeds in them. (Navel oranges, bananas, seedless grapes, etc. have had the seeds bred out of them. Use fruits with seeds.)

Each kind of fruit has its own kind of seeds.

Question: Does one kind of fruit have different kinds of seeds in it? Place several of the same kinds of fruit (cut open) together on a table. Repeat for a variety of fruits. Have the children compare the seeds from fruits of the same kind with those from other kinds of fruits.

Some fruits have only one seed; others have many.

Question: How many seeds do different kinds of fruits have? Cut open several different kinds of fruit and lay them on the table. Have the children compare them as to the number of seeds each contains.

Seeds

Not all seeds look the same. There are many different kinds of seeds.

Question: How are seeds different from each other? Show different kinds of seeds. Let the children compare them and tell you their differences in terms of size, shape, color, and number.

Seeds of different kinds of plants are different in size, shape, color, and number.

Most plants have seeds; some plants do not.

Question: Do all plants have seeds? Show several plants that have seeds. Then show several that do not (ferns, etc.). Place the plants in two groupings. Ask the children which group has the most plants. In the autumn, take the children for a walk and point out plants that will never have seeds. Let them see how many they can find that do produce seeds.

Each kind of plant has its own kind of seeds.

Question: Does one kind of plant have different kinds of seeds? Show several mature seeds from the same plant. Have the children examine several plants of the same kind, then seeds from another kind of plant or plants. Try to get them to tell you that each plant has its own kind of seed.

Seeds help us to tell one plant from another. We can sometimes tell what kind of plant we are looking at by its seeds.

Question: Can we tell what kind of plant we are looking at by its seeds? Bring a variety of annual plants to school. Each plant should have mature seeds. Tell the children the name of each plant as you show it and its seeds. Then see how many of the plants they can identify by looking at the seeds only.

B. There are many different kinds of plants

People take care of some kinds of plants they grow in yards, parks, along streets, and in orchards; others grow wild without people caring for them.

Question: Do people take care of all plants we see? Take the children for a walk to see plants in yards, parks, along streets, etc. Then take them out to the country to see wildflowers, trees, and shrubs.

The differences in plant parts help us to tell plants apart.

Question: How can we tell plants apart? Let the children compare different kinds of plants as to roots, stems, leaves, fruits, flowers, and seeds. See how many they can tell apart from the others and how many they can name.

Trees

Trees do not all look the same.

Trees are not all the same size.

Different kinds of trees have different kinds of leaves, bark, and flowers.

Question: How do trees differ from each other? Let the children compare pictures of different kinds of trees. Take them out to look at trees. Have them compare the trees in height, width, size of trunk, leaves, flowers, etc.

Evergreen trees, which usually have narrow or scale-like leaves, have cones.

Question: What kind of seed containers do narrow-leaf trees have? Show a variety of conifer branches, each with its own seed cones. Let the children compare the leaves of the cone-bearing trees with some that do not have cones—maples, ash trees, etc.

C. Plants grow to be different sizes

Some plants are small; others are big.

Question: How much difference is there in the sizes of plants? Show pictures illustrating different sizes of plants. Take the children for a walk and have them compare the sizes of the plants they see.

D. Some plants live longer than others

Some plants live for many years, some for two seasons, and some for only one season.

Question: How long do plants live? For a long-term project, plant some annual (one season to seed) seeds and some biennials (two seasons to seed), i.e., carrots, near some long-lived perennial plants. Let the children see that the annuals die at the end of the summer or earlier; the biennials die at the end of (or before) the following season; and the perennials do not die, but keep on growing from year to year.

E. Some plants do not have any seeds

Some plants like algae, mosses, etc. do not have seeds.

Question: Do all plants have seeds? Show different kinds of algae, mosses, liverworts, ferns, and horsetails. Have the children look for seeds and discover that there are none.

Some plants are not green.

Question: Are all plants green? How are molds different from other plants? Grow some bread mold by dampening a slice of bread that has been exposed to the air and placing it in a covered dish. Leave the dish in a warm, dark place for several days until a mold forms. Have the children compare the mold with a green plant. Focus their attention on the color. Show some brown and red seaweeds and have the children compare them with a green plant.

Mushrooms do not have any green color.

Question: Are all plants green? How is a mushroom different from other plants? Have the children compare a mushroom with a green plant. Focus their attention on the lack of green color in the mushroom and the fact that the mushroom has no roots, stems, leaves, or flowers.

Molds do not have any leaves, stems, or roots.

Question: How are molds different from other plants? Have the children examine bread mold and compare it with a green plant. Focus their attention on the absence of leaves, stems, and roots.

Mosses are not all the same in size and shape.

Question: Are all mosses the same? Show a variety of mosses (or pictures of mosses). Let the children compare them as to size and shape.

Ferns are not all the same in size and shape.

Question: Are all ferns the same? Repeat the activity above for ferns.

F. Plants are alive

*Plants are different
from things that
are not alive in
some ways.*

Question: How do we know that plants are alive? Place a potted plant on one end of a table and several inanimate objects on the other end (rocks, pieces of metal, etc.). Have the children compare the plants (living things) with rocks, etc. (non-living things). Lead the children in a discussion of differences, i.e., plants grow and take in water; the others do not.

G. Plants and animals are different in some ways

*We can tell plants
from animals.*

Question: How are plants different from animals? Show a potted plant and a live animal (dog, kitten, etc.). Have the children compare them. Lead them in a discussion of the differences, i.e., plants do not move about, etc.

H. Plants and animals are alike in several ways

*Plants and animals
both take in food and
water, grow, etc.*

Question: Are plants like animals in any way? Discuss the similarities between plants and animals, i.e., both take in water and food, both grow, etc.

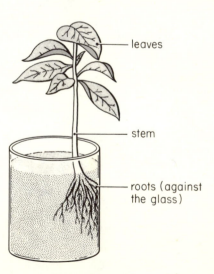

$$\large 3$$

Plant Structure and Function

A. Plants have different parts, and each part is useful in a different way

Roots

Roots are the part of the plant that grows under the ground.

Set a small plant that clearly shows roots, stems, and leaves in a jar of soil. Place the plant against the glass so that the parts can be seen easily. (If a carrot is used, remember that only an old plant that is preparing to bloom will have the stem.) Name the three

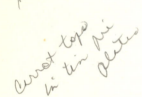

leaves

stem

roots (against the glass)

parts—root, stem, and leaf. Ask, "Which part of the plant is under the soil?" Take the children outdoors to see growing plants. Pull up several small plants. Ask, "Which part of the plants was under the ground?"

Plants take in water through their roots.

Pull up a cheeseweed plant, or some other succulent plant, by its roots or buy a carrot with the shoot intact. Remove the outer skin of the root by peeling or scraping. Immerse the root of the plant in a jar of water to which red food coloring has been added. (Blue coloring must be used for a carrot plant. To ensure absorption, the root must be cut cross-wise and the cut end be thrust into the dye solution for twenty-four hours. Then cut the root and stem length-wise down the middle. The water-conducting tubes will be stained red (or blue). Ask, "Which part of the plant did the food coloring enter?"

Pull a cheeseweed plant up by the roots or secure some other soft-leaf plant. Let the plant dry until the leaves are severely wilted. Now have the children observe how the leaves regain their former firmness within the next few hours by placing the root in a glass of water and leaving it for a time. Ask, "Where did the water that made the leaves spread out again get into the plant?"

Some plants store food in their roots.

Show different kinds of plant roots that we eat—carrots, turnips, etc. Prepare some food from these roots for the children to eat.

Cut a potato in half. Show the children some iodine solution. Say, "The color of this iodine is yellow [or brown]." Place a drop or two of the iodine solution on the cut surface of the potato. Ask, "What happened to the color of the iodine when I put it on the potato?" Say, "Yes, it is changed to blue-black." Tell them that iodine changes color when it touches starchy food and that this shows that the potato has starch in it. Test other foods such as bread, crackers, etc. and discuss the color changes with the children.

Some plants have roots that do not grow in the ground, but are used for climbing.

Show sections of vines such as English ivy, Boston ivy, Virginia creeper, etc. that have aerial roots extending from their stems. It may be necessary to tell the children that these are roots. Now take the children for a walk to see vines growing. Focus their attention on the clinging roots.

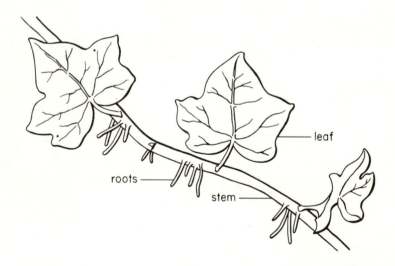

Stems

Plants have stems.

The stem is the part of the plant that is between the roots and the leaves.

Show a variety of plants. Hold up a plant and point out and name the parts that are above ground, i.e., stems, leaves, etc., and the part that is below ground, i.e., roots. Have the children come, one by one, and point out the stem of each plant. Ask,

Most stems are above the ground. Branches hold the leaves and flowers.

"What part of the plant is between the roots and the leaves? What part is above the ground? What do the branches have on them?"

Some stems are under the ground.

Show white potatoes (tubers), onions (bulbs), gladioli (corms), and ferns and iris (rhizomes). It will be necessary to tell the children that these are the kinds of stems that grow under the ground. (Don't use sweet potatoes. They are true underground roots.)

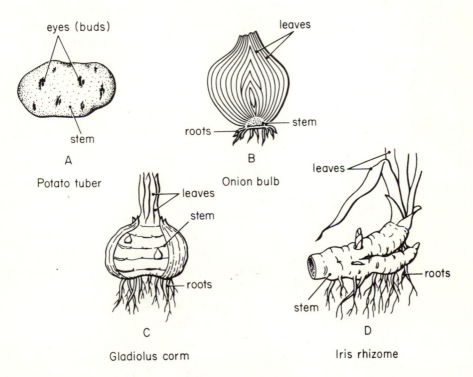

eyes (buds)

stem

A

Potato tuber

leaves

roots — stem

B

Onion bulb

leaves

stem

roots

C

Gladiolus corm

leaves

roots

stem

D

Iris rhizome

Underground stems

Sprout a white potato by wrapping it in wet paper and placing it in a warm spot. After the "eyes" have sprouted, show the potato to the children. Point to the sprouts and say, "These are little branches that have grown from the potato stem. Most branches grow from stems above the ground, but potatoes are stems under the ground."

Most stems that are above the ground hold leaves out to the light.

Tell the children that they are to pretend that they are stems. Hang a paper "sun" from the ceiling. Have them stand under the "sun." Give each child two paper "leaves" to hold in his hands. Tell them to stretch out their "branches" (arms). Direct the "wind" of an electric fan toward the children and let them wave their "branches" and "leaves" in the "wind." Say, "Look at the 'sun.' Why do trees and other plants hold their branches and leaves out in the air away from the trunks of trees or plant stems?"

Show a broad-leaf potted plant such as a coleus, geranium, etc. Hold the plant under the light. Ask the children to point out the stem and leaves. Ask, "How does the stem help the leaves to get light?"

We can see the path that water travels when it goes up inside the stem.

Place the roots of a cheeseweed plant or a cut stalk of celery in a jar of cold water to which red food coloring has been added. (Actually the celery we eat is not a stem, but the stalk (petiole) of a leaf which rises from a short stem near the ground.) Leave the plant in the food coloring for twenty-four hours. Then cut length-wise through the leaf stalk. Let the children see the red-stained tubes where the water went up into the stalk. Ask, "Where did the water go up the stem? How can we tell?"

The stem of a tree is made of three

Show cross sections of tree branches that are about six inches long. Use branches, *parts—the bark, the sapwood, and the heartwood.*

such as elm, which have dark center (heart) wood. Point out and name the bark, light sapwood, and the dark center heartwood. Point to the position of the cambium (growing layer) between the bark and the sapwood. Explain the function of the cambium. Now have the children name the three parts as you point them out on different branches. Show a cross section of a branch. Help the children draw the three layers and color them.

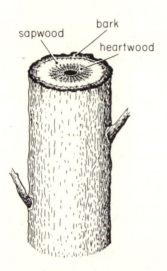

The outside layer of a tree is called bark. Bark protects the inside of a tree.

Have one child pretend to be the inside of a tree. Give a second child, who pretends to be the bark, a shield to hold on his arm. Have a third child try to hit the "inside of the tree" with a rolled-up paper "stick." Let the child with the shield, who is pretending to be the bark of the tree, protect the "inside of the tree." Ask, "How does the bark help the tree?"

The sapwood is just under the bark and is light-colored.

Show cross sections of tree branches. Point out and name the sapwood. Now have the children point out and name the sapwood on other branch sections as you hold them up.

The inside wood in many trees is dark in color. It is called heartwood.

Repeat the previous activity for heartwood.

The stems of some plants are protected by thorns.

Show stems of roses, bougainvillea, etc. that are covered with thorns. Ask, "How do the thorns help the plant?"

Some stems can climb.

Let the children plant pole beans or peas and watch the plants climb by twisting about the supporting sticks or poles that you have set up. Take the children for a walk to show them various kinds of climbing vines, i.e., English ivy, Virginia creeper, creeping fig, etc. Ask, "What can the stems of these plants do that the stems of other plants such as trees or shrubs cannot do?"

Some plants send out stems called runners that grow along the top of the ground.

Show the children samples of strawberry plants, Bermuda grass, and other plants that send runners along the top of the ground or just under the surface. Plant several strawberry plants in a corner of the schoolyard. Let the children watch the development of the runners and the new plants that form on the ends of the runners. Set up an aquarium. Plant eel grass (Vallisneria) obtained from a pet shop. Let the children watch the plants reproduce by sending out runners along the surface of the sand.

Buds

Buds are found on stems.

In winter show a variety of twigs of broadleaf trees that have lost their leaves. Point out the buds. In spring or summer show a variety of branches. Pull off several leaves and point out the buds which are located in the angle (axil) where the branch and leaf stalk join. Have the children look for buds on other branches and point out the buds to you. (Don't use conifers, of course.)

Buds have leaves or flowers, or both leaves and flowers inside them.

During the winter, collect a variety of twigs with buds on them. Wrap the twigs in wax paper and then in newspaper, and place them in the refrigerator (but not in the freezing compartment). Branches of fruit trees, i.e., apple, peach, pear, etc., will have some buds that contain only leaves; others, only flowers; still others, like walnut, have buds from which both leaves and flowers emerge. During the spring when buds are opening, take the twigs out of the refrigerator and place them in jars in the room. Have the children watch the buds open up, revealing leaves and (or) flowers. (Almonds, apricots, and peaches in California bloom from middle to late winter according to the calendar. "Calendar seasons" and "growth seasons" often do not coincide. This is important for the children to know.)

Buds protect the leaves and flowers that are inside them.

Repeat the previous activity. Ask, "How do the bud coverings help the leaves and flowers inside them?"

Leaves

Plants have leaves.

Leaves are fastened to the stems.

Show several kinds of leafy branches. Ask, "What do all the branches have on them? To what part of the plant are the leaves fastened?"

Leaves have several parts. Most leaves

Show a leafy branch. Pick off a leaf. Point out and name the parts of a leaf. Hold up *have stalks that attach them to the stem and a flat blade.*

other leaves. Ask, "Which part of the leaf fastens it to the branch? Can you point to the stalk?"

Show the children some leaves. Ask, "The blade is what part of the leaf?" Help them to realize that it is the wide, flat part. Ask, "Can you point to the blade of this leaf?"

Leaves have veins in them.

Show several leaves in which veins appear clearly. Then show other leaves and ask, "Can you point to the veins in this leaf?" Help the children to learn that the veins are the lines in the leaves.

The veins of the leaf carry water in the leaf.

Place the stalks (petioles) of several leaves in a glass of water to which red food coloring has been added. Leave them there until the veins have become stained red. (Some leaves will absorb the coloring more quickly than others. You will have to watch for the right time to show them to the children.) Ask, "What part of the leaves carries the water? Through what part of the leaf does the water go?" Point to the veins of the leaf where the red coloring is being absorbed.

Leaves are usually green.

Show leafy branches. Ask, "What color are the leaves?" Tell them that leaves are usually green.

Some leaves have other colors besides green in them.

Show leaves of coleus, variegated ivy, etc. which have different colors.

When a leaf falls off a twig or is picked off, it leaves a scar which shows where the leaf has been.

Obtain some branches of tree of heaven, elm, oak, horse chestnut, buckeye, maple, etc. Have the children pick off leaves. Focus their attention on the places on the branches where leaves have been attached.

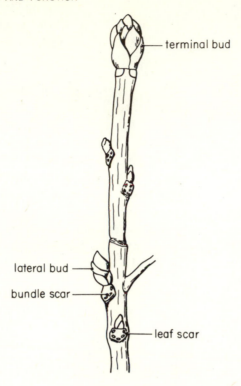

terminal bud

lateral bud

bundle scar

leaf scar

Ask, "How can we tell where a leaf was fastened to the branch? Can you point to a leaf scar on this twig?"

Flowers

Flowers come out of some of the buds of plants.

During the winter, gather twigs of fruit trees. Select branches with buds on side spur twigs. Wrap these branches in wax paper and newspapers and put them in the refrigerator. When warm weather comes, place the branches in jars of water on a table. Let the children enjoy watching the buds open and the flowers emerge. (Don't judge spring by the calendar; judge it by plant behavior. If you wait longer than February (winter) in some localities, the flower buds will be open on trees out of doors. Almonds in California commonly bloom by mid-February; apricots, shortly afterwards; then, peaches.)

Fruits

Flowering plants have fruits.

Bring in branches of plants with flowers and fruits in different stages of development. Point out the developing fruits in flowers on which the petals still remain. Take the children for a walk to see trees and bushes which they have observed earlier and which now have fruits. Recall to the children's minds the fact that the plants had flowers when last observed. Ask, "What do plants with flowers make when the flower petals drop?"

There are seeds inside fruits.

Show several different kinds of fruits. Cut some of them open. Ask, "What do fruits have inside?" Point to a seed.

Pods are fruits because they have seeds inside them.

Bring in pods of wisteria, lupine, Oriental poppies, peas, beans, etc. Ask, "Are these fruits? How do we know?" Help the children to understand that we call them fruits because they have seeds inside them.

Pine trees have cones with seeds.

Gather pine cones which are mature but still unopened. Place them in a box on the table. As they dry, they will open up and release winged seeds. (This is not true of the closed pine cones which must be opened by heat or by mechanical means.)

Some parts of plants that we call vegetables are really fruits.

After the lesson in which the children learn that anything with seeds inside is really a fruit, show several plant foods that are fruits, but commonly called vegetables, such as tomatoes, bell peppers, etc. Remark that people call these vegetables. Ask, "What are they really? Why?"

Seeds

Plants grow from seeds.

Have the children plant different kinds of seeds and watch the plants sprout and grow.

Seeds are made inside flowers.

Have the children grow different kinds of garden plants such as squash, peas, beans, etc. until the plants produce fruits. Ask, "In what part of the plant are the fruits with their seeds made?" Show the different stages of development.

EXPLORING, COMPARING, AND SEEING RELATIONSHIPS

A. Plants have different parts, and each part is useful in a different way

Roots

Plants have roots.

Question: What part of the plant is the root? Show different kinds of plants. On one plant, show the part that is above the ground. This is the shoot (stems and leaves). Point out and name the part that is under the ground (roots). Examine and compare the known plant with the other plants. Have each child point out and name the roots on each plant.

Some plants have one central (tap) root with many small roots; others have many roots but no central (tap) root.

Question: What two types of roots do plants have? Place a carrot at one end of a table and a grass (or corn) at the other. Place a mixed group of plants between them. Have each child come to the table, pick up a plant and place it with either the carrot or the grass, depending on whether or not the plant has a tap root (carrot) or a mass of fibrous roots (grass).

Roots hold (anchor) the plant in the ground.

Question: What keeps a plant from falling over? Place one carrot against the glass in a clear glass or plastic container that has been filled with soil so that the whole plant is clearly visible. Cut the top from another carrot at earth level and plant it in another glass in the same way. Now have a child push against the top of each carrot (or turn on an electric fan, directing the current of air against each carrot in turn, to represent the wind). Ask, "Which plant blew over—the one with the root or the one without the root? Why didn't the plant with the root blow over? Why did the plant without the root blow over?"

Stems

Some plants have rings in the wood; others do not.

Question: Do all plants have rings in the wood? Show examples of cross sections of trees which clearly show rings in the wood —oak, maple, any conifer, etc. Also show cross sections of such plants as palms, corn, etc. which do not show rings. Have the children compare the two types. Ask, "How are the insides of this type different from the insides of the other?"

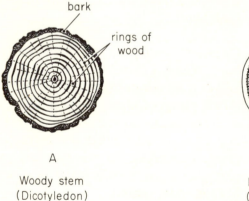

A

Woody stem
(Dicotyledon)

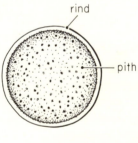

B

Non woody stem
(Monocotyledon)

Trees grow by adding layers of wood each year.

Question: How can we tell if a tree is growing older? On a sheet of paper draw two cross sections of stems showing rings (layers) of growth—one with six to eight rings; the other, with three to four rings.

Have the children count the number of rings on each tree stem that you have drawn. Now show them a cross section of a stem that clearly shows the rings. Help them to count the rings as far as they can count. Tell them that each year the tree grows enough to make one ring. Have them compare the stems (one actual stem and one that you have drawn on paper). Ask, "Which tree is older—this one with three or four rings, or this one with six or eight rings, or this real one? How can you tell?"

Some stems are green; some are not.

Question: Are all stems brown? Show green stems. (The tip shoots of nearly all plants are green, especially when they are young. Have the children compare these stems with other stems that are not green.)

Some stems are stiff; some are soft and bend easily; some break easily.

Question: Are all stems stiff? Show some stems that are stiff and others that are flexible. Show some that are brittle and snap easily. Let the children feel the stems and try to bend and break them. Have them talk about the differences in stems.

Buds

Buds usually open in the spring.

Question: When do buds open? Take the children for a walk during the cold winter months. Focus their attention on the closed buds on deciduous trees. When the weather has warmed enough, take them out again to see how the buds which they observed in winter have opened up; or show spring branches from the trees on which the buds have opened up.

Buds open up when the weather becomes warm.

Question: What makes the buds open? During the winter, gather branches of deciduous trees with the buds tightly closed. Store these in the refrigerator after wrapping them in wax paper and then in newspapers. Have the children put their hands into the refrigerator to feel how cold it is. Ask, "How does it feel?" As soon as the weather warms up, remove the branches from the refrigerator. (In California in a warm year, this may be even before Christmas. Acacia blossoms early; almonds do too. Watch for signs on the trees.) Focus the children's attention on the fact that while the buds on the trees outside are open, those in the refrigerator are still closed. Now place the branches in jars in a warm sunny window. Draw the children's attention to the warmth of the room. Talk about the cold of the refrigerator. Have them observe the opening tree buds. Ask, "How are the room and the refrigerator different? What made the buds open?"

Flowers

Some plants have flowers; others do not.

Question: Do all plants have flowers? Show a variety of plants, some, such as grasses, ferns, and mosses, without visible flowers; others, with showy blossoms. Place a plant without blossoms at one end of a table; a plant with flowers at the other. Have the children place the rest of the plants in one group or the other according to whether or not they have flowers.

Some flowers grow in clusters; others grow alone.

Question: Do all plants have just one flower on a stem? Show many kinds of flowers, some with single blossoms, others with flower clusters. Have the children compare and group the unknown plants with the two known plants as in the previous activity, i.e., flowers versus no flowers.

Some flowers

Question: Do all flowers smell sweet? Re-

*are fragrant; others
are not.*

peat the previous activity, but call the children's attention to the fragrance of the flowers of the different plants.

Fruits

*There are seeds
inside fruits.*

Question: How can we tell a fruit from a vegetable? Arrange a variety of fruits in a row on a table. Besides an apple, orange, avocado, etc., include a bell pepper and a tomato. Cut each fruit open. Now have the children compare each fruit with the others. Ask, "In what way are nearly all fruits the same?" Be sure that the children understand that it is because fruits have seeds.

Seeds

*A seed is made
of seed coats, a
baby plant, and
stored food.*

Question: How can we tell a seed? Make an artificial bean seed out of styrofoam. Cut and shape the styrofoam to the form of a lima bean. Cover the outside with paint, paper, modeling clay, etc. to represent the seed coats. Cut the "seed" in half length-wise. In the proper position on one of the two styrofoam sections (as determined by examining a real lima bean seed), fasten a plant cut from paper or cloth. Now lay the two halves of the seed side by side

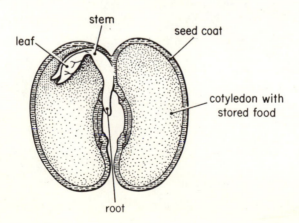

on the table. Show the children this "seed" and point out and name the parts—seed coats, baby plant, and stored food.

A seed has a baby plant inside.

Question: Besides the stored food, what does the seed have inside it? Soak large lima beans, horse beans, or other large beans for twenty-four hours (or thirty-six hours, if necessary) until soft. With your fingernail or knife, split the beans open on the rounded side and carefully spread apart the two halves. Have the children examine the two halves. Point out the seed coats, stored food (in the cotyledons), and the baby plant (embryo) and name them. Have the children compare their seed with the artificial one. Get them to point out and name the parts of the real seed, if they can, and the corresponding parts of the artificial seed. Soak several large lima beans in water as before. Again split the seed open carefully on the rounded side. Spread the two halves apart. Carefully remove the half which does not hold the embryo plant. Point to the embryo and tell the children that this is a baby plant. Now place the half of the bean seed containing the plant in a glass or peanut butter jar about one to two inches from the top, with the side of the seed holding the embryo pressed tightly against the glass. Fill the inside of the glass with soil or cotton, etc. Wet the soil or cotton. Let the children observe the development of the roots and shoots from the embryo plant, thus proving that this structure was indeed a baby plant.

B. Some plants are not green

Not all plants are green.

Question: Are all plants green? On a table, place a green plant. Beside this put a non-green plant, i.e., mold, mushroom, etc. Ask, "How are the plants different?" Talk about the colors and let the children examine the plants. (In this activity do not consider leaves, stems, roots, etc.) Now give the children several plants to compare with the two types on the table. Have them place each plant with one or the other of the two plants on the basis of color.

C. Plants adjust their structure and function to their environment

Plants that live under water have soft stems that bend easily.

Question: How are the stems of plants that live under water different from plants that live on land? Show several plants that live under water, either salt or fresh water. Have the children feel them and bend them. Now show several land plants more rigid in structure. Have the children try to bend them also. Ask, "How are the stems of water plants different from the stems of land plants?" Explain that some land plants also have soft stems, but that most land plant stems are stiffer than those of water plants.

Some plants that live in the desert have thorns to protect them from being eaten by animals.

Question: How do plants that live in the desert protect themselves from being eaten by animals? Show a thorn-covered cactus. Have the children compare it with an ordinary woody garden plant as to means of protection from animals.

Some plants that live in the desert store water inside themselves.

Question: How do cactus plants that live in the desert keep from drying out and dying from lack of water? Show a barrel cactus or a prickly pear. Cut a section from the cactus and squeeze fluid from the inner pulp. Now show a section of a tree stem. Show that the inside part is woody, without any readily visible fluid.

4

The Relation of Plants to Man

A. We use plants

*We use plants in
different ways.*

Show the children a variety of colorful
pictures of farm animals feeding in a pasture, families enjoying the beauty of their
gardens, parks, or picnic areas, people picking fruit in orchards, lumbermen felling
trees, etc. Discuss with the children the
many ways plants are useful to people.

Show many kinds of products we get from
plants. Select those in which the plant material is most clearly visible. Encourage the
children to bring to class articles made of
plant material.

Food

*Some of our food
comes from plants.*

Show different kinds of plants used for food
and foods made from plants. Ask each child
to bring to class samples of food plants or
canned or packaged foods made from
plants, such as corn flakes, peanut butter,
canned fruit, etc.

Plants give us fruits and vegetables.

Show different kinds of market vegetables: leaf—cabbage, lettuce, chard, spinach, etc.; root—carrot, radish, beet, etc.; stem—asparagus, bamboo shoots, etc.; and bud or blossom—artichoke, cauliflower, etc.

Plants give us sugar and syrup.

Obtain some sugar cane and let the children chew the pith. Let them chew and taste a piece of sugar beet. Tell them that we get sugar from sugar cane and sugar beets, but the sugar must be extracted and purified, because sugar isn't all that these plants contain.

Crush a sugar beet or piece of sugar cane. Heat the juice to evaporate the water until a thick syrup is formed. Have the children taste the syrup. Show sugar in granular or cube form. Tell or read the story of how sugar is made.

Certain trees give us maple syrup and maple sugar.

Take the children to see a sugar maple tree in a yard or park. (Sugar maple trees are grown, especially in the East, as ornamentals in many parks and along streets.) Or show a picture of a sugar maple tree that is being tapped for its sap. Let the children taste some maple syrup and maple sugar candy. Tell them that the sweet juice that came from the tree into the pail, when boiled down and filtered, becomes the syrup. (The commercial product has cane sugar in it too.)

Bees get a sweet juice called nectar from flowers. They use this nectar to make honey.

Let the children watch honey bees fly from flower to flower. Have some honeysuckle flowers or other tubular-throated flowers such as verbena, etc. on hand. Let the children suck the stem ends and taste the sweet nectar. Buy a section of comb honey. Tell the children that the sweet juice of the flowers is gathered by the bees, changed into honey, and stored in the cells of the comb. Let the children taste the honey.

Plants give us seasonings for our food.

Show bay leaves, cinnamon bark, parsley, dill, mint, sage, oregano, etc. Prepare a food that contains some seasoning in its whole form so that the children can see the seasoning in the food.

Some trees give us fruits and nuts.

Take the children to a place where they can see nuts and fruits growing on trees. Bring in twigs or small branches with nuts and fruits on them.

We eat many different kinds of plants.

Show different kinds of plants that people eat, such as spinach, beets, chard, carrots, etc. Show the whole plants if possible. Discuss others.

We eat different parts of plants.

Bring in a variety of whole plant vegetables. Let the children see that each plant has roots, stems, and leaves, all of which we eat. As you show each plant, ask, "What part of this plant do we eat?"

We may get several different kinds of foods from a single plant.

Show the children different kinds of foods made from the same plant. Prepare food in different ways, using the same plant, such as corn, beans, etc. Encourage the children to bring different kinds of commercial foods prepared from one plant, such as corn flakes, hominy, cream-style corn, corn on the cob, etc., or instant mashed potatoes, potato chips, frozen French fries, etc.

We eat the seeds of some plants.[1]

Show corn on the cob, beans and peas in pods, etc. Cook them and let the children eat them. Encourage the children to bring to class samples of seeds that people eat.

We eat the seeds of some grasses.[2]

Secure several stalks of oats, barley, wheat, corn, rice, etc. Remove the husks from the seeds. Cook the seeds and let the children taste them. Show some grain and husks secured from a local feed store.

We grow different kinds of grasses for food.

Obtain stalks of different kinds of grains. Husk out several seeds from each kind. Show grocery store packages containing these different kinds of grains.

We make food from plants and from parts of plants.

In the presence of the children, prepare a fruit or vegetable salad made from different parts of plants. (Lettuce leaves, celery, carrot curls, cauliflower buds, olives, orange sections, etc. can be used.)

Many kinds of plants are grown for food in gardens and on farms.[3]

Show colored pictures of food plants growing in gardens, orchards, or on farms. Have the children tell of their own experiences in growing vegetables or watching adults work in gardens. Take a field trip to an orchard or truck garden.

Some mushrooms are good to eat.

Buy some fresh mushrooms from a grocery store. Cook the mushrooms in butter, season them with salt, and let the children taste them. (Tell the children why they must never eat any mushrooms they find growing

---

[1] The children should have learned previously that a seed is a baby plant together with stored food and a seed coat.

[2] The children should have been taught earlier to recognize grasses. Grasses have long, narrow leaves with the bottom parts always wrapped around their hollow stems.

[3] The children should have learned earlier to recognize fruits and vegetables.

in the yard or elsewhere. Take the children to visit a mushroom farm, if possible.)

Foods we get from plants help us to grow.

Help the children to understand that foods we get from plants help us to grow. Encourage them to eat different kinds of foods from plants.

We need foods we get from plants to help us live.

Discuss with the children how foods from plants help them to stay alive—that when they feel hungry, their bodies are needing food.

Some animals eat plants.

Have the children watch various kinds of mammals and birds—cows, horses, guinea pigs, rabbits, canaries, chickens, etc.—eat plants. If individual children have plant-eating pets at home, let them describe the kinds of plants their pets eat.

Clothing

We make clothes out of parts of some kinds of plants.

Show articles of wearing apparel that are clearly made of some plant material—straw hats, fiber belts, straw sandals, etc. If possible, show the plants so that the children can see what parts are straw, where the fibers are in flax, etc.

Shelter

We use wood from trees to make houses and other buildings.

Show pictures of houses in process of construction. Take the children to see a house being built. Show a picture of a tree being

cut into boards. Secure a section of a tree branch (about six inches in diameter). Get a carpenter to slice this branch length-wise into several boards. Show the children that the tree was cut into boards like those used in building houses.

We use some kinds of plants for shelter.

Show various ways in which we use plants to protect us from the wind, sun, rain, etc., such as trees planted for windbreaks, for shade, etc.

Medicines

Plants give us some of our medicines.

Show different kinds of medicines made from plants—white pine cough syrup, horehound and honey drops, etc. Show the horehound plant, if it grows in your community. If possible, let the children taste the cough syrup or horehound and honey drops.

Paper

Paper is made from wood.

Rub some balsa wood (which may be obtained from a hobby shop) on the fine part of a vegetable grater until sawdust is produced. Mix the sawdust with a small quantity of starch; then mix with water to the consistency of soft dough. Let the children use a rolling pin to roll out the dough on pieces of wax paper. When the "paper" is dry, let them mark on it with crayon. Tell them that it is "play paper," that real paper is also made of wood, but in a different way.

Perfume

Perfumes are made from flowers and sometimes the wood, e.g., myrtlewood, of some plants.

Place the blossoms of fragrant flowers such as roses, gardenias, lilacs, carnations, etc. on the table. Encourage the children to enjoy their fragrance. Then show them samples of floral perfumes, soaps, etc. having the same fragrance as the flowers they have smelled. Explain that the fragrances in commercial products come from flowers.

B. We use plants in many other ways

*We use many
different kinds of
seeds and things
made from seeds.*

Show many different kinds of useful seeds—peanuts, corn, beans, sesame seeds and poppy seeds used in baking, mustard seeds for mustard, etc.

*We get useful things
from trees.*

Show different products made from wood, bark, leaves, and seeds of trees—boards, cork, gum, resins, fibers, Presto logs, etc.

Recreation (pleasure)

*It is fun to grow
plants.*

Have the children plant some seeds and care for the growing plants. While the children are working, show your enjoyment and say, "Isn't it fun to plant seeds and help them grow?"

*People have fun in
the forest during
vacations.*

Have the children describe their vacations in forested areas. Show pictures of people vacationing in places where there is a profusion of grass, trees, etc.

Beauty

*Plants—trees,
shrubs, grass, and
flowers—make
homes, parks, streets,
gardens, and high-
ways more beautiful.*

Show colored pictures of homes, public gardens, and highways planted with trees, flowering shrubs, beautiful lawns and flowers. Talk about ways we can use plants to make our homes, cities, and highways more beautiful.

Jobs

*People's need for
plants makes differ-
ent kinds of work for
many people.*

Show colored pictures of foresters, orchardists, farmers, nurserymen, gardeners, etc. at work with plants. If possible, show motion pictures of these professions or take the children to visit an orchard, nursery, flower seed farm, etc.

C. Animals use plants

Food

Some animals eat plants or parts of plants.

Show colored pictures of cattle, sheep, or horses grazing in a pasture, deer eating tree leaves, squirrels eating nuts, birds and chickens picking up seeds, etc. Talk with the children about their experiences seeing animals eat or helping to feed them plants or plant parts.

Shelter

Plants are useful to animals as homes, shelter, and hiding places.

Show colored pictures of plant-animal relationships—birds making nests in trees, raccoons, squirrels, or woodpeckers looking out from holes in tree trunks, and birds and other animals hiding in grass, shrubs, or trees. Tell them that a bare yard has no birds. Place a hollow branch or section of a tree trunk in a cage with pet hamsters, laboratory rats, etc. Let the children see the animals hide inside the trunk. Tell the children that you are going to take them outside to watch the birds and you want them to see where the birds go when they see the children.

D. Plants help to make soil better

Molds help to make good soil out of dead plants by causing them to decay.

Show pieces of wood or bark that are crumbling from mold growth. Point out the white mold on the wood. Tell them that dead wood and leaves make good food for plants.

E. Some plants can harm us

Poisonous plants

Some plants or their parts have poison in them and can harm us.

Show pictures of mushrooms, leaves and flowers of oleanders, and seeds and leaves of castor beans, leaves of poison oak or poison ivy, and other poisonous plants

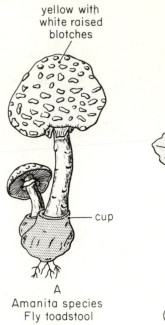

yellow with
white raised
blotches

cup

A
Amanita species
Fly toadstool
(mushroom)

trifoliate
leaf

B
Poison oak
(Western United States)

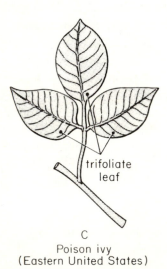

trifoliate
leaf

C
Poison ivy
(Eastern United States)

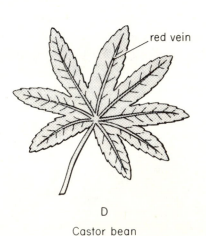

red vein

D
Castor bean

prevalent in the community. Make sure the children recognize these plants and their identifying parts. Caution them against touching or eating any part of these or other injurious plants. Caution them also against picking or eating any kind of mushrooms they see growing out of doors.

Poison oak (or poison ivy) is a harmful plant.

Discuss with the children the symptoms of poison oak (or poison ivy) poisoning. Let any who have had such poisoning tell their experiences or the experiences of their families or friends who have had it.

Other harmful plants

Some plants are harmful to other plants.

Show pictures (or the actual plants, if possible) of mistletoe growing on other plants. Show plants or pictures of shelf or bracket fungi growing on trunks of trees. Tell the children that the mosses and lichens they see on trunks and branches of trees do not harm the trees.

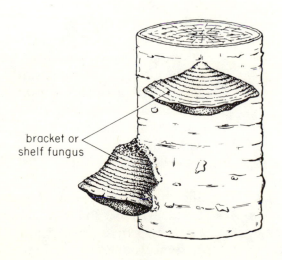

bracket or
shelf fungus

Weeds are harmful plants.

Take the children into the yard or a vacant lot to look at weeds. Tell them that a weed is any plant that grows where people do not want it to grow. A plant may be a weed in one place and a flower in another.

Some weeds are so tall that they keep the sunlight away from other plants.

Take the children for a walk. Show them tall plants and short plants growing together. Focus their attention on how the tall plants keep the shorter ones from getting any sunlight.

Let the children plant a number of tall-growing plants and short-growing plants together in a box. Let them observe how the tall plants shut off the light from the shorter ones.

Some plants (molds) make food spoil.

Show a moldy orange, lemon, or grapefruit. Have the children place it in a covered dish and in contact with a mold-free citrus fruit. The dish should be kept in a warm, dark place. Let the children observe how the mold spreads to the healthy fruit. Give the children small pieces of bread which have been rubbed on the floor or table. Have them moisten the bread and place it in a covered dish in a warm, dark place. Let them see how the mold spreads over the bread and spoils it. Have the children mix some clear Knox gelatin with a small quantity of hot water (one envelope of gelatin to one half cup of water). Pour into dessert dishes and set in a dark place. A growth of mold will form on the gelatin in a few days.

Some plants (molds) give a good taste to some foods.

Show the children some Roquefort cheese. Let them taste it and tell them that it is liked by many people. Or make a salad and put on some Roquefort dressing. Let them taste it.

*Some molds give
us medicine.*

Show the children some penicillin tablets.
Talk about how people are made well by
taking antibiotics prescribed by doctors.
Tell them that penicillin, etc. is made from
certain kinds of molds.

Control of harmful plants

*People have different
ways of keeping
harmful plants from
hurting them or
hurting animals or
other plants.*

If the children have a garden spot of their
own, let them hoe or pull weeds. Show
pictures of people hoeing or burning weeds.
Take the children outside and show them
daisies, dandelions, or similar broad-leafed
plants in lawns. Spray or dust with a weed
killer, letting the children watch from a distance. (Use Weed-B-Gon, WeedDone, etc.)
Over the next several weeks, have the children look at the plants each day and see that
they gradually turn yellow and die. Caution
them about the dangers of touching sprayed
material or putting their fingers in their
mouths after touching sprayed leaves or
branches.

F. Some plants eat insects

*A few kinds of
plants catch and
eat insects.*

Set up a small terrarium. Let the children
plant one or more carnivorous plants. (The
plants and soil can be purchased from a
biological supply house).[4] Venus fly-trap is
the most satisfactory. Catch and kill several
flies. Drop a fly or other small insect onto
the open leaf trap. Let the children watch
the two halves close over the fly.

*Plants that eat
insects catch them in
different ways.*

Purchase a pitcher plant. Cut one of the
leaves of the plant in two length-wise. Show
how the pitcher plant drowns insects in its
central cavity.

---

[4] General Biological Supply House, Chicago; Ward's Natural Science Establishment,
Rochester, New York (branch office, Cannery Row, Monterey, California); Carolina Biological Supply House, Chapel Hill, North Carolina.

A
Leaf of Venus fly trap

B
Pitcher plant

G. Plants make baby plants that look like themselves

Plants make new plants like themselves.
Each kind of seed makes the same kind of plant as the one that made it.

Bring in different plants—beans, corn, etc. which contain ripe seeds, together with stems and leaves. Let the children plant the seeds and watch the plants grow. Have them observe that each kind of seed produces a plant like the plant from which the planted seed came.

H. We should protect trees, flowers, and other useful plants

Most wildflowers should be left where they are growing to make seeds for next year and for other people to enjoy.

Take the children on a trip to see wildflowers. Since all children should have the happy experience of gathering wildflowers, teach them to pick them carefully and in moderation, and not to pick any rare species.

Pulling up wildflowers by the roots kills them.

Have the children pull annual flowering plants by the roots. Lay the plants on the table. After several hours or the next day, have the children note that the flowers have wilted. Try to get them to express the idea that wildflowers should be left where they are found growing to make seeds for next year's plants.

Fires kill trees, wildflowers, and other plants.

Show pictures of leafless blackened trees, the result of a forest fire. Place a potted plant (geranium, etc.) on the ground. Pile some straw around the pot and light the straw. Let the children observe that the fire killed the plant.

We should watch our campfires when we go camping so they will not burn trees and other plants. We should plant trees to take the place of those that have been burned or cut down.

After the previous experience, draw from the children expressions as to the importance of watching campfires and carefully putting them out after we are through with them.

Show pictures of crews of men reforesting cut-over or burned land. Discuss with the children burned forests they have seen and what they can do to prevent such waste.

We should plant trees to make our cities, parks, and other places beautiful and to give us shade.

Help the children to plant a seedling tree in the school yard. Talk with them about how they can help to care for it.

We should take good care of our useful plants.

Show pictures of farmers, gardeners, or orchardists, etc. caring for plants. Take the children to see a gardener or other adult caring for plants. Let them take care of certain plants in the school yard—watering, fertilizing, etc.

Greenhouses protect plants from cold.

On a cool day in winter, take the children to a commercial or private greenhouse. Help them notice how much warmer it is inside the greenhouse than outside.

Lath houses protect plants from too much sun and from getting too dry.

Show pictures of lath houses and plant shelters. (These are sometimes covered with plastic or cheesecloth.) Take the children to visit a nursery. Let them ask the nurseryman why he has a lath house.

Plants have many enemies that harm them.

Bring to class branches of plants that have been damaged by insects or fungi. Take the children for a walk to look for plants that have been damaged in the same way. If possible, have them see insects or their larvae in the act of eating plant leaves.

Some insects and molds are harmful to plants and we must kill them by spraying them with poison.

Show pictures of plants being sprayed for insects or fungi (molds, etc.)

Garden pests, such as insects and molds, eat or kill different parts of plants.

Bring to class for the children to examine roots, stems, leaves, flowers, fruits, and seeds of plants showing insect or fungus damage.

EXPLORING, COMPARING, AND SEEING RELATIONSHIPS

A. We use plants

Food

We eat some kinds of plants—their roots, stems, leaves, flowers, and fruits; some kinds are not good to eat.

Question: Can we eat every kind of plant? Bring to class several kinds of fruits and vegetables that can be eaten raw—apples, peaches, grapes, etc. and carrots (make carrot curls) and celery (make celery sticks), etc. Bring also several kinds of inedible but harmless plants—wood stems, leaves, flowers, etc. Have the children bite on the different items and tell which plants tasted good and which did not.

Fruits are the seed containers of plants; vegetables are the roots, stems, seeds, and flowers of plants.

Question: What is a fruit? What is a vegetable? Bring a variety of fruits to class—an orange, bell pepper, tomato, pear, apple, avocado, etc. Cut each fruit in half. Have the children compare them. Ask, "How are these fruits alike?" They should tell you that they contain one or more seeds. Now show a variety of edible roots, leaves, etc. Have the children compare these with the fruits. Ask, "How are these roots, stems, and leaves different from fruits?"

We get tea from plants.

Pour boiling water over some tea leaves and allow them to steep, first having flattened several of the tea leaves to show the children what they are like. Have them compare them with similar plant leaves of other kinds. Tell them that some people make tea out of other such leaves—camomile, alfalfa, mint, etc. Let them taste the tea.

We get coffee from plants.

Question: From what is coffee made? Secure some whole coffee beans. Let the children compare these beans with red kidney beans or lima beans. Show pictures of coffee plants with beans.

We eat some kinds of mushrooms.

Question: Are all mushrooms good to eat? Buy some whole mushrooms. Cut up some of them and cook in butter with a bit of salt. Let the children taste them. Warn the children that they must never eat any wild mushrooms they find growing outside because some are poisonous and will hurt them.

Mushrooms do not have any green color.

Question: How are mushrooms different from other plants? Show green plants and let the children compare them with mushrooms.

Prevention of soil erosion

Plants help to keep the soil from being washed away by water (rain) or blown away by wind.

Question: What happens to soil when it rains if we take all of the plants out of the ground? Fill two bread (or similarly shaped) pans with soil. Completely cover the soil in one bread pan with a piece of grass turf. Place each pan separately in a larger container with one end of each pan raised.

Have the children fill a sprinkling can (or a milk carton with a number of holes punched in one end) with water. Let them pour the same amount of water on the upper end of each bread pan. Have the children compare the amount of soil washed off the surface of each pan. Ask, "Why is it important to keep plants growing in the soil?"

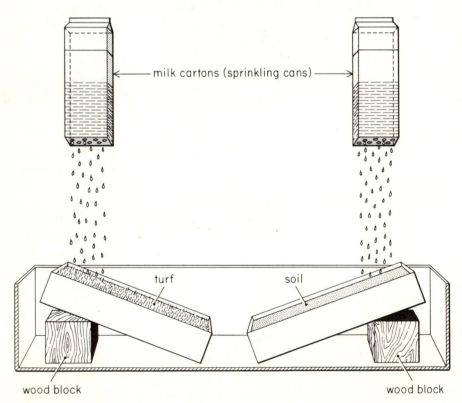

milk cartons (sprinkling cans)

turf   soil

wood block   wood block

Ask: What happens to the soil when the wind blows, if we take all of the plants out of the ground? Place two piles of dry soil on a large piece of paper, each pile consisting of one half soil and one half leaf mold. Cover one pile with a piece of dry turf. Now have the children blow on each pile (or turn on an electric fan or hair dryer). Then have them compare the amount of soil blown away from each pile. Ask, "Why is it important to keep the ground covered with growing plants?" Show pictures of hillsides that have been eroded by water or wind action. If it is a rainy day, show them the muddy water running in the gutters; or take them for a walk to observe roadside cuts or areas cleared for housing where there has been rain to cut gulches; or to the beach to see sand dunes, if the weather is fair. Show pictures of hillsides covered with trees and shrubs or other vegetation. Help them to understand why the soil is held in place by the roots of vegetation.

Enrichment of soil

Plants help to make soil better for growing plants.

Question: What kind of soil is best for making plants grow? Secure two small flower pots (or wax paper cups with several holes punched in the bottoms). Fill both pots (or cups) with powdered glass or clean washed sand. To one pot (or cup), add some leaf mold or a little peat moss. Help the children to plant two sprouted seedlings of the same kind and size in the pots. If bean or corn seedlings are used, be sure to remove the food-filled seed leaves (cotyledons). Water the plants with distilled water only. (Distilled water may be secured from a local service station.) When the two plants show distinct differences in growth (the plant in leaf mold should be larger), show them to the children and ask, "Which plant grew the most—the one that grew in the sand or the one in sand mixed with the dead plant leaves [leaf mold]? Why, then, do you think people mix dead and rotted plants with the soil in which they grow plants?"

Molds help to make good soil out of dead plants by making them decay.

Question: Do molds help us in any way? Show two kinds of wood—one, sound; the other, crumbling and containing mold growth. Let the children examine and handle both. Have them crumble some of the rotting wood, then mix it with some soil in a box or pan. Have them fill two flower pots as in the previous activity, one with sand only; the other, with sand and rotted wood, and grow some plants. As in the previous activity, this will require several weeks, but the children can be encouraged to watch the plants and compare the growth.

Beauty

Plants and flowers make our homes, gardens, streets, and parks more beautiful.

Question: How can we make our gardens, streets, and parks more beautiful? Show colored pictures of well-planted gardens, streets, and highways. Show other pictures of home gardens, parks, etc. that are poorly planted or completely bare. Take the children for a walk in the schoolyard and around the neighborhood. Let them compare well-planted grounds with those that are poorly planted or that have no plants at all.

B. Some plants can harm us

We can learn to to know poison oak (or poison ivy).

Question: How can we tell poison oak (or poison ivy) from other plants? Show pictures or outline drawings. Show branches of bushes, vines, or trees that grow in the same environment as poison oak (or poison ivy). Have the children compare the leaves of poison oak (or poison ivy) with other leaves. Repeat until every child can identify the harmful plants. Now take the children to a location in which poison oak (or poison ivy) grows. Let each child find and point out the harmful plants. Both poison oak and poison ivy have a trifoliate leaf, i.e., a leaf with three leaflets, and they have a bushy habit of growth. Poison oak is common to the western part of the United States. Poison ivy is a more variable species with a bushy or climbing habit. The leaves are smooth and glossy like those of poison oak, but may be hairy, entire, toothed, or lobed. It is common to the eastern and north-eastern parts of the United States. Caution the children about touching either of these plants.

We can learn to know castor bean plants.

Question: How can we tell castor beans from other plants? Show pictures or outline drawings of castor beans or, if possible, branches of the plant, together with pods and seeds. Show branches of various kinds of bushes, vines, and trees that grow in vacant lots or roadside areas where castor beans are apt to be found. Have the children compare the castor bean leaves with leaves of other similar plants. Help them to recognize the pods and seeds as well as the leaves. Caution the children never to put any part of the plant in their mouths.

We can learn to know oleander shrubs.

Question: How can we get to know oleander shrubs? As in the activity above, teach the children to recognize this shrub. It is often planted in parks, home gardens, along highway strips, and along streets. It is a beautiful flowering shrub, but it is poisonous.

C. Some kinds of plants (molds) spoil our foods. Some foods must be kept from spoiling in some way; other foods are prepared so that they do not need to be kept from spoiling

We can keep foods from spoiling in several different ways.

Question: How can we keep foods from spoiling? Prepare two dishes containing fresh sliced apples, pears, figs, etc. Place one dish in the refrigerator; the other, in a warm spot. Show the two dishes to the children each day for several days. Ask, "Which dish of food spoiled? Why didn't the food kept in the refrigerator spoil?" Have the children put their hands inside the refrigerator and feel the cold. Ask, "How is the inside of the refrigerator different from the outside?"

Prepare four dishes of food. In one, put some perishable fruits or vegetables. In the others, put some dried, salt-cured, and sugar-cured foods. Place them side by side in a warm room. Show them to the children every day for several days. Ask, "Which food spoiled? Which did not spoil? How was the food that did not spoil different from the food that did spoil?"

D. We must protect and take care of our useful plants

We should take care of the trees that grow wild and those that we plant in our yards, along the streets, in parks, and along highways.

Question: How can we take care of our plants? Take the children to see trees that have been treated by a tree surgeon (or show pictures). Have them compare the treated trees with trees that have been attacked by fungus or rot and not treated.

Greenhouses protect plants from cold; so do lath houses.

Question: Why do people put plants in a greenhouse? Place a small potted plant (with tender leaves) in the freezing compartment of the refrigerator until the leaves are frozen. Let the children compare this plant with one that has been kept in a warm, sunny window in the classroom. Ask, "Why was the plant in the refrigerator hurt?" Now show pictures of healthy plants in a greenhouse or take the children to visit a greenhouse on a cold day. Ask, "How does a greenhouse help to keep plants healthy?"

Question: How do lath houses protect plants? Take the children to visit a lath house. Ask the owner to explain how the lath house protects his plants from too much sun.

We must protect our useful plants from insects by spraying them or dusting them with poison.

Question: How do we protect our useful plants from harmful insects? Take the children into the schoolyard or elsewhere, where they can see harmful insects or their larvae on the plants and resultant plant damage. Or bring to class branches with live aphids (plant lice) on them and other branches that had them but have been treated by dusting or spraying with poison. Do not let the children touch the branches, but have them compare the appearance of the healthy and unhealthy plants. Ask, "What did the poison spray or dust do to the aphids?"

Now show branches with live aphids or their larvae or adult forms of other insects on them. After the children have seen the live insects, spray one set of branches, using a Flit spray gun. (Do this out of doors and at a distance from the children.) After an hour, let the children observe the results. Ask, "What did the poison spray do to the insects [or larvae]?"

Some of the poison sprays we use to kill harmful plants do not hurt the plants we want to keep.

Question: Can we kill weeds without killing the good plants we want to keep? Locate two dandelion plants on the school lawn. Water one of them with a solution of Weed-B-Gon or WeedDone. Do not allow the children to get any of the solution on them. Water the other dandelion with plain water. Let the children observe the plants every day for two or three weeks. The poison-treated dandelion should turn yellow and die; the grass around it should stay green. (If the lawn is affected by oxalis, a plant with a small clover-like leaf, use Kansel powder instead of Weed-B-Gon or Weed-Done.)

E. Plants make baby plants like themselves

A plant that grows from a seed looks like the plant that made the seed.

Question: Does each kind of seed make only one kind of plant? If we plant the seeds from a certain plant, what will the baby plants look like? Let the children plant several kinds of seeds—radishes, beans, annual flowers, etc. in a flower pot or box, or a spot in the schoolyard. Let the children care for the plants until they produce seeds. Re-plant the seeds. Let the children see that the offspring look like the parent plant. (This is a rather long-range project for very young children, but the teacher can use the activity without difficulty if, when the children are planting the seeds, she says, "I am going to keep some of these seeds and we'll see if they are like the seeds your plants make when they get big, or whether they are different." Put the seeds into a brightly colored container and help the children to remember. When the children's plants produce seeds, show them the seeds you have saved and let the children compare them.

5

The Relation of Plants to Their Environment

A. Different kinds of plants grow in different kinds of places

Some plants grow in deserts where the sunshine is hot and there is very little water.

Show pictures of plants growing in deserts— cactus, date palm, sagebrush, mesquite, century plant, etc. Obtain a small barrel cactus or prickly pear cactus. Cut it open to show that water is stored inside.

Some plants live in the ocean.

Show pictures of seaweeds. Focus the children's attention on the ways seaweeds are adapted to environmental conditions along the seashore, i.e., they have flexible stalks, soft tissues, and air sacs to help them float, etc. Take the children to the beach. Encourage them to look for and examine different kinds of seaweeds. Back in the classroom, mount seaweeds on construction paper in the following manner. Place a piece of construction paper on the bottom of a pan. Wash the seaweed with fresh water and place it in a water-filled pan. Float the seaweed into the desired position on the paper. Then lift the paper slowly and drain off the excess water. Cover the seaweed with a layer of cheesecloth. Then place the construction paper with the seaweed on it between several thicknesses of newspapers. Lay the newspapers on the floor, place a flat board on top, and put a heavy weight on top of the board. Each day for three or four days, change the newspapers that are on each side of the construction paper that has seaweed on it. Remove the cheesecloth with the first change of paper. In a week or so, the mounts should be dry. The smaller, more delicate varieties of seaweed are, of course, best for this activity.

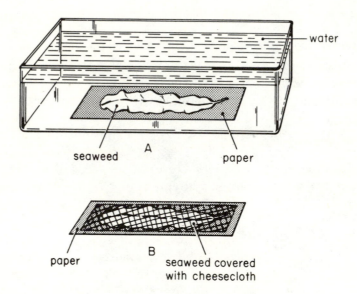

seaweed   A   paper

paper   B   seaweed covered
                          with cheesecloth

Some plants live under water in streams and ponds.

Collect and show various kinds of algae and higher plants which grow under water in streams and ponds. Set up an aquarium in the classroom. Stock it with various kinds of underwater plants—Vallisneria (eel grass), Myriophylum (hornwort), Elodea, etc. Set up another container and stock it with various kinds of underwater algae. Take the children for a trip to a stream or a pond. Show them water plants growing in their natural environment. Focus their attention on the ways underwater plants are adapted to their environmental conditions in stream or pond, i.e., soft flexible stems, etc.

Some plants grow in shady places.

Show pictures of plants living in canyons or other shady places. Collect and show samples of plants that live in shady places. Take the children for a trip to a shady canyon; if this is not possible, show them plants such as philodendron or rubber plants growing inside buildings. Show them also plants that grow under other plants on the school grounds or in shady places.

Some plants live in marshy places.

Show pictures of plants—lilies, cattails, sedges, etc.—living in marshy places.

B. Factors of the environment affect plants

Temperature

Too much cold kills plants.

With the children watching, place a potted plant (small begonia, philodendron, or similar plant) in the freezing compartment of the refrigerator. The next day, show the plant to the children.

Too much heat kills plants.

With the children watching, place a potted plant in the oven and turn on the heat. Later take the plant out and let the children see that the heat killed the plant. Let them plant and care for a potted house plant during the winter months. Place the plant in a well-lighted window. After a freezing night, call their attention to the fact that the plant is healthy because it has the right amount of heat.

Water

Rain gives water to plants.

During a rain, call the attention of the children to the fact that the rain has soaked and is soaking the soil, thereby helping the plants to grow. (The children should already have learned that plants need water.)

Too much water kills some plants.

Place a potted begonia plant in a pail of water for two or three weeks. The plant should gradually sicken and die. (Some kinds will just grow extra roots all up and down the stems. Use a plant that will not do this.)

Too little water kills plants.

Place a potted plant in a sunny location. Every day have a child give it a teaspoon of water, or less, so that it will die.

Light

Leaves of plants turn toward the light.

Place a potted plant (geranium, etc.) in a sunny window. After a few days, the plant will bend toward the light. (The effect may be noticeable overnight.)

Plants grow toward the light.

Start a climbing bean plant (Kentucky Wonder, etc.) in a two- or three-inch pot. Place the pot in a shoebox to which card flaps have been attached. See illustration. The box should be painted black inside and should have a hole in the top. For another variation of this experiment, place a potted bean plant in a box which has a hole in one end. The inside of the box should be painted black or covered with black paper to absorb light. The plant will grow toward the lighted opening.

Green plants turn yellow and die if they cannot get light.

Place a short board on the lawn. After about two weeks, lift the board and show the children how the grass under the board has

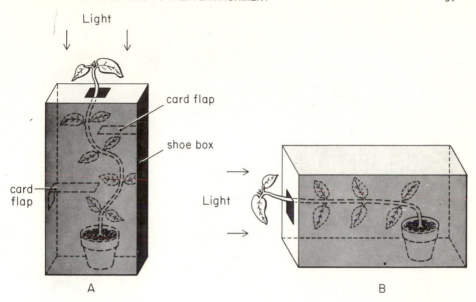

turned yellow. A week or so later, return to the same spot and show the children how the yellow patches have turned green again. Place a potted plant in a dark closet (or box) for a week or two. At the end of the time, the plant should have yellowed considerably.

Enemies

Plants have insect enemies that harm them.

Show pictures of plants with insects or their larvae eating the leaves. Show pictures of molds (fungi) on trees and other plants. Bring to school branches of plants that have insects or fungi (molds, mildew) on them or that show insect or fungus damage.

C. Seeds are scattered in several ways

Some seeds are scattered by the wind.

Gather seeds of milkweed, oyster plant, dandelion, maple, elm, etc. Let the children throw the seeds into the air and watch them settle down again or fan them through the air with pieces of cardboard. Take the chil-

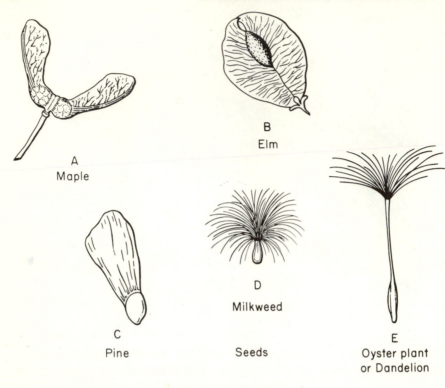

A
Maple

B
Elm

C
Pine

D
Milkweed

Seeds

E
Oyster plant
or Dandelion

dren for a walk to find seeds that are carried by the wind.

Some seeds are scattered by floating on the top of water.

Gather seeds of dock. Let the children scatter these on the surface of a pan of water. Take them for a walk to see dock plants growing along ditches or in fields that have been covered by an overflow of water.

Some seeds are scattered by catching on the clothes of people.

Gather seeds of cocklebur, foxtail, etc. Let the children wearing sweaters or wool clothing brush against a branch of cocklebur or foxtail, etc. and see that the seeds remain caught on their clothing. Take the children for a walk to find seeds that catch on their clothing.

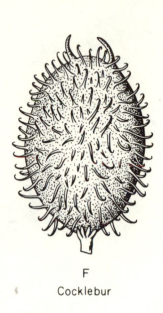

F
Cocklebur

G
Fox-tail

Some seeds are scattered by catching on the fur of animals.

Gather seeds of cocklebur, foxtail, etc. Bring a cat, dog, or rabbit to school. Let the children place seeds against the fur of the animal or brush a cocklebur against the fur of the animal.

Some seeds are scattered by dropping out of their seed containers onto the ground beneath.

Show ripe pods of peas, beans, honeysuckle, marigolds, nasturtiums, lupines, mustard, radish, or plants of the mint family. Let the children break open several pods and watch the seeds drop to the ground when the pods are opened.

Some seeds are scattered and planted by people.

Show various crop seeds, i.e., corn, melon, etc. Discuss how people might take their seeds to different places and plant them. Discuss how seeds might be scattered by people when they are driving cars. Show pictures of farmers or gardeners planting seeds.

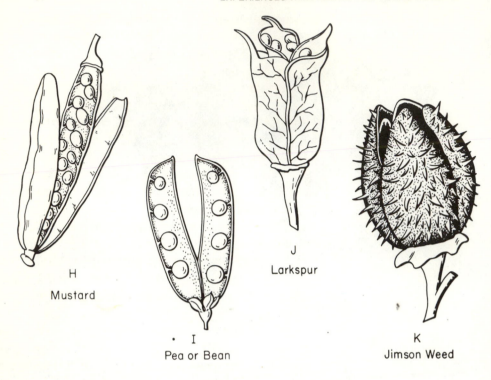

H

Mustard

I

Pea or Bean

J

Larkspur

K

Jimson Weed

Plants stay in one place, but their seeds can be scattered to different places and make new plants there.

Show a picture of a large tree or plant with seedlings growing nearby. Take the children for a walk to see young plants growing near the parent plants. (This experience should follow those in which the children learn that seeds are scattered by the wind, water, fur of animals, clothing of people, etc.) Ask the children, "Does the parent plant move? Then how did these baby plants get to be where they are? Look at the seeds of the parent plant." Demonstrate how the seeds are scattered, i.e., by wind, water, on clothing of people, fur of animals, etc. If it is not practical to take the children outside, dig up a cocklebur or oyster plant and set it in a flower pot. Be sure that the plant has ripe seeds. Plant two or three young plants in small pots. Set these eight or ten feet from the large plant. For cocklebur, foxtail, etc., whose seeds are carried by people and animals, let one of the children rub against the large plant and get burs on his clothing. Now ask, "How did the baby plants get here if the parent plant cannot move?" For dandelions, oyster plants, etc., whose seeds are carried by the wind, let the children throw seeds into the air. Ask, "How did the baby plants get over here, if the parent plants cannot move?" For dock or other plants, whose seeds may be carried by floating on water, let the children float the seeds on a pan of water. Ask, "How did the baby plants get here if the parent plant cannot move?" For peas, beans, corn, nasturtiums, marigolds, etc., whose seeds are usually planted by people, let the children plant seeds in small flower pots. When the seeds have sprouted, place the pots eight or ten feet from the parent plant and ask, "How did the baby plants get here, if the parent plant cannot move?"

D. Pollen is carried from flower to flower by insects

Pollen is carried from one flower to another by honey bees and other insects.

Show pictures of honey bees carrying pollen or hovering over flowers. (In the pollen season, bees carry pollen on their hind legs or dusted over their bodies.) Take the children outside and let them watch bees flying from flower to flower. Focus their attention on the pollen in the pollen sacs on the bees' hind legs and the pollen which has been dusted over their bodies.

EXPLORING, COMPARING, AND SEEING RELATIONSHIPS

A. Different kinds of plants grow in different kinds of places

Some plants grow in gardens, along streets, in orchards,

Question: Are all of the plants we see cared for by people? Show pictures of plants growing in well-kept gardens and parks, along

*or on farms where
people take care of
them; others grow
wild and no one cares
for them.*

streets, in orchards, etc. Show other pictures
of wildflowers, trees, shrubs, etc. Stress the
fact that the first group is cared for by
people, while the second group does not get
any care. After taking the children for a
walk to a park or garden, take them out to
the country to see wildflowers, trees, shrubs,
etc. growing wild. (A good lesson on self-
reliance might be taught in connection with
this experience.)

B. Factors of the environment affect plants

Temperature

*Plants can be grown
in the house in
winter because it is
warm there.*

Question: Why can we grow plants inside
the house sometimes when we cannot grow
them outside? Let the children plant and
care for a potted house plant. Place the
plant in a well-lighted window. After a
freezing night, call the children's attention
to injured plants outside. You might place a
philodendron, begonia, or geranium outside the window the night before. Let the
children contrast the uninjured plant in-
doors with the injured plant or plants outside.

*Too much cold kills
plants.*

Question: What happens to some plants
when the weather becomes very cold? Show
two healthy plants (philodendron or geranium) having tender leaves. (Use two plants
of the same kind.) Let the children put their
hands into the freezing compartment of the
refrigerator to feel how cold it is. Now place
one of the plants in the freezing compartment and let it stay there until it is clearly
damaged. Show the two plants to the children. Ask, "What was it that hurt the plant
that was in the refrigerator and caused its
leaves to shrivel?"

Too much heat kills plants.

Question: What happens to some plants when the weather becomes very hot? Show two healthy plants as in the previous activity. Turn on the heat in an oven. Let the children stand in front of the oven to feel the heat coming out. Place one plant in the oven until the leaves are clearly damaged. Have the children contrast the two plants. Ask, "What was it that hurt the plant in the oven and made its leaves shrivel up?"

Too little heat keeps plants from growing.

Question: What is one reason why plants do not grow very well in the winter? During the coldest part of the winter, sprout some garden pea or bean seeds in two flower pots that have been placed in a warm, sunny spot (on the window sill) in the classroom. Now put one pot outside in a cold, shady location. Give both pots the same amount of water. Have the children compare them from week to week. Call their attention to how cold the weather is outside. Say, "The plants outside and inside got the same amount of water. Then why did the plant inside grow and the one outside not grow?"

Water

Much water kills some plants.

Question: What happens to some plants when we give them a great deal of water? Show two healthy plants that are growing in pots. Submerge one in a pail of water or fill the top of the pot with water several times a day. Have the children observe the plants for several weeks. Ask, "Why is the plant deep in the water dying?" Help them to understand that plants can drown, too. Or soak Transvaal daisies in the school yard with water day after day and have the children watch them die from over-watering.

Too little water kills some plants.

Question: What happens if we give a plant very little water? Show two healthy potted plants of the same kind. Place them side by side in a warm sunny spot. Let the children give one plant a normal amount of water; the other, only a teaspoonful or less every other day. Ask, "What makes this plant [that did not get much water] not grow as well as the other plant?"

Some plants need more water than others.

Question: Do all plants need the same amount of water to grow well? Get two potted plants — one, a drought-resistant plant, i.e., cactus, succulent, or woody, thick-leaved shrub; the other, a soft thin-leaved shade plant, i.e., philodendron, etc. Place the two plants together in a warm sunny spot. Have the children give each plant a cup of water every two weeks. Then have them compare the appearance of the two plants.

Ask, "Which plant looks better when it is given water only once every two weeks? Then which plant needs water more often?"

Plants and the Seasons

A. Plants change with the seasons

Autumn

Some plants change when the cold weather comes.

Take the children for a walk. Let them see how the leaves on some trees and shrubs are changing color and dropping off.

Trees that lose their leaves before cold weather comes have buds on their branches for next year's leaves and flowers.

Bring to class branches of a deciduous tree that has brightly colored leaves. Have the children pick off the leaves and observe that where a leaf has been picked off, a bud is usually left. Take the children to see deciduous trees. Have them locate the buds in the axils of the leaves, i.e., the angle between the leaf stalk and the twig. Next spring, take the children back to see how the buds have opened up to produce leaves and/ or flowers.

Plants that live for only one season make seeds before they die.

Take the children for a walk and locate some dead plants (annuals, i.e., plants that produce seeds and die the same year). Let them find seeds on these plants, scattered beneath the plants or the husks from which the seeds have dropped.

The leaves of many trees and shrubs change color in autumn.

Take the children for a walk in autumn. Show them trees that you took them to see in the spring or summer, but whose leaves have now changed color.

Many leaves change color in the autumn because the green color goes away.

Cut leaves out of construction paper or thin cardboard. Paint the leaves to represent fall-colored leaves. Spray the painted leaves with clear plastic spray. Now cover the plastic surfaces with green water color or poster paint. Have the children wipe off the green color with a damp sponge or cloth. This activity will help the children understand that the colors of many autumn leaves are exposed by the disappearance of the green chlorophyll.

Winter

Scars on the branches in winter show us where the leaves were fastened to the branches in the spring and summer.

Show bare branches of trees which have prominent leaf scars (tree of heaven, horse chestnut, and California buckeye are good for this purpose. The California buckeye often loses its leaves in midsummer.) Take the children to see a tree they have already observed earlier in summer and early autumn. Have them look for any marks on the twigs that might show where the leaves have been.

Spring

Buds open up in the spring.

Take the children for a walk in the spring to see the same trees that they observed in the autumn and winter. Focus their attention on the opening spring buds. Cut twigs of buckeye or horse chestnut in winter. Store the twigs in the refrigerator. In the spring, place them in containers of water and let the children watch the buds swell and burst open. (Willow and elderberry leaf out early in the spring; some trees leaf out in late

winter. Some trees (walnuts) wait until late
spring or early summer to leaf out.)

Trees that drop their
leaves in winter grow
new leaves in spring.
All trees grow new
leaves in spring.

Continue observing buds on a selected tree.
Watch the new leaves develop. (New leaves
never grow in the places where there were
leaves before.)

Seeds sprout in the
spring.

Plant some seeds in a box or flower pot. Let
the children watch the seeds sprout and
grow. (Seeds sprout whenever they have
water in California, other western states,
and in the South.)

Plants start to grow
in the spring.

Take the children for a walk in the spring
to visit the same place they visited in the
winter. Focus their attention on signs of
plant growth. (In California and other
places noted above, they start to grow when
they have water.)

Summer

Many fruits get ripe
in summer.

In the late spring, take the children to an
orchard or garden that has fruit trees or
berry vines. When harvest time comes, return to the same place and help the children
to gather some ripe fruits. Discuss with them
the times when fruits get ripe. (In California, there are fruits that ripen all the way
from May to September. Variety and non-
conformity to rules are typical of California
plants.)

EXPLORING, COMPARING, AND SEEING RELATIONSHIPS

A. Plants change with the seasons

Plants look different
in autumn, winter,
spring, and summer.

Question: Do trees look the same all
through the year? Select a broad-leaf (pref-
erably a fruit tree such as apple, peach, etc.).

Show Film

Let the children observe the changes it goes through during the year. Show colored pictures of the changes undergone by a single tree during the year. Ask, "How does the tree look different in the fall from the way it looked in summer? How does it look different in the winter from the way it looked in the spring?"

Different plants have flowers at different times of the year.

Question: Do different kinds of plants have their flowers at the same time? Let the children observe and keep a record of the blooming times of different kinds of plants on the schoolground. (This sometimes depends on the planting and watering times.)

A garden looks different at different times of the year.

Question: How does a garden look different at different times of the year? Have the children visit a garden once a month to observe the changes that take place in the plants. (In California, if there is a mild winter with no frost, some plants may keep actively growing all through the winter. When there is frost, the frost determines the season.)

Some plants (trees) drop their leaves in autumn.

Question: In late autumn or early winter, how is the color of most of the leaves of plants that drop their leaves in winter different from the color of those that keep their leaves? Take the children for a walk, focusing their attention on evergreen trees and deciduous trees. Recall the fact that the deciduous trees were covered with leaves earlier in the year. Have them compare the deciduous trees with the evergreen trees.

Evergreen trees drop their leaves all through the year.

Question: Do evergreen trees drop their leaves all at the same time? Where on the branches do the new leaves grow? Several times during the year, take the children to see an evergreen tree (redwood or fir) growing. Let them observe that, though the ground is covered with many dead leaves, the tree is still full of green leaves. If the children examine the tips of the branches, they will find this year's needles near the tips and the older needles farther back.

Nearly all narrow-leaf trees keep their leaves in autumn and winter.

Question: Do all trees look the same all the year? Ask, "How do some trees look during the autumn? Do they have any leaves? Which trees—those that keep their leaves in the winter or those that drop their leaves in winter—have the narrow leaves?"

If broad-leaf trees keep their leaves in autumn and winter, the leaves are usually thick.

Question: How are the leaves of the wide-leaf trees that keep their leaves in winter different from the leaves of wide-leaf trees that lose their leaves? Show branches of coast live oak, camellia, etc. These plants keep their leaves through autumn and winter. Let the children examine the leaves and compare them with the usually thin leaves of such deciduous plants as maple trees, Weigelia, etc.

Trees that lose their leaves in autumn show buds on their branches for next year's leaves and flowers.

Question: Which trees—those that keep their leaves in winter or those that drop their leaves—show buds when the leaves are pulled off? Bring to class branches from an evergreen coniferous tree, i.e., fir, pine, etc. and branches from a deciduous tree, i.e., maple, etc. Have the children locate the buds. Show them that the evergreen tree does not show any lateral (or side) buds when the leaves are pulled off, while deciduous trees do. (Evergreen coniferous trees as a rule never have lateral buds, though they do have terminal buds on the tips of their branches.)

Plants that die in autumn make seeds for next year's plants.

Question: How do plants that die in autumn, or when winter comes, make sure that there will be new plants of the same kind next year? Take the children for an autumn walk. Locate some dead annual plants. Compare these annual plants with nearby seedless green bushes. Ask, "Which plants have seeds?" Explain to the children that other plants make seeds, too, but because they die when winter comes, the plants that die (annual plants) must make seeds for next year's plants.

Conditions Needed for Germination and Growth

A. Plants need certain conditions to germinate and grow

Soil

Seeds can be made to sprout without soil because they have food stored inside them.

Have the children place an assortment of seeds (radish, bean, corn, nasturtium, etc.) between two pieces of wet cloth. Put the seeds in a covered dish. After several days, let the children see the sprouted seeds.

Soil air

Soil has air in it.

Water pushes the air out of soil.

Fill several glasses half full of very dry soil. Then let the children fill the glasses with water. Show them the bubbles coming out of the soil.

Water

Some plants need very little water to grow.

Get a cactus or other succulent plant. Keep it in the classroom for several weeks. Do not water the plant during this time. Call the children's attention to the fact that the plant has not been watered, but still looks healthy.

B. We must prevent and control weeds, insects, and plant diseases that harm our useful plants

We must keep weeds, insects, and plant diseases from hurting our useful plants.

Show pictures of people caring for house plants, plants in the garden, parks, etc. Take the children for a walk to see well-cared-for gardens, people working in gardens or orchards and caring for plants in different ways.

Plants in our houses, parks, along our streets, in orchards, and on farms need care, i.e., watering, weeding, cultivating, and spraying to grow well.

See previous activity.

Plants in our yards, parks, orchards, and on farms need to be sprayed with poison to get rid of weeds, insects, and diseases that would harm them.

Show pictures of people spraying or dusting plants to destroy weeds, harmful insects, and plant diseases. Take the children to a place where they can see plants being sprayed or dusted with poison. Encourage them to ask questions of the person doing the spraying or dusting. (Care must be taken to keep the children out of harm from the spray.)

EXPLORING, COMPARING, AND SEEING RELATIONSHIPS

A. Plants need certain conditions to germinate and grow

Soil

Seeds sprout better in soft soil. We should make the soil soft before we plant our seeds.

Question: When we want to make seeds sprout well, does it make any difference whether the soil is soft or hard? Set up two jars filled with soil. Plant seeds between the soil and the glass sides of both jars so that the seeds are clearly visible. With the children watching you, pack the soil down *very hard* in one jar; in the other, pack it *very loosely*. Have the children observe that in the jar in which the soil has been packed down very hard, the shoots of the baby plants have difficulty in coming up and the roots have a hard time going down. Ask, "Before we plant seeds, what should we do to the soil so that the little new plants can come out of the soil and their roots go down easily?" Perform the same experiment again, but in place of the hard-packed soil use soft soil. Plant the seeds between the soil and the glass where they are clearly visible. (Be sure to pack the soil down *very hard* in one jar; in the other, pack it very loosely.)

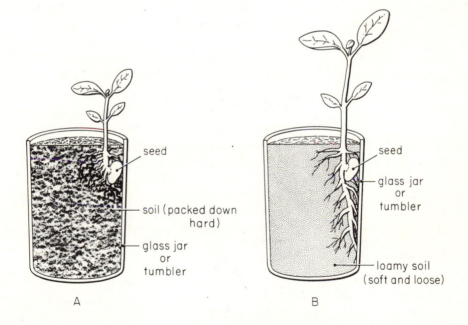

seed

soil (packed down hard)

glass jar or tumbler

A

seed

glass jar or tumbler

loamy soil (soft and loose)

B

Plants grow better if they have soft soil.

Question: Do hard soil and soft soil make any difference in the way a plant grows? Plant two small plants in flower pots. (Plants should be of the same kind.) Pack the soil down *hard* in one pot, but not the other. Be sure that the soil is level with the tops of the pots so that any water that is not absorbed will run off. Have the children water both plants equally, but sparingly. Have them observe the growth and condition of the plants for several weeks. Ask, "Which kind of soil—hard or soft—takes in water better? Which plant looks and grows better? What must the soil be like if plants are to grow well?" Perform the same experiment, but plant two of the same kind of plants—beans, corn, etc. in glass jars so that the roots are visible against the glass. Trim the roots back one-third their length before planting. Set one plant in clay soil; the other, in garden loam enriched with peat moss. Pack the clay down hard, but not the loam. Have the children observe the growth and condition of the two plants for several weeks. Ask, "In which soil—clay or loam—are the roots better able to move? Then, which soil is better for plants?" (In long-term exercises, the teacher can help the children set up plants, but she should also prepare another set earlier which will show the results in a short time.)

Water

Seeds need water to sprout.

Question: What do seeds need to sprout? Place paper cylinders in two tall peanut butter jars. Have the children fill the center of each jar with either sawdust, cotton, peat moss, or vermiculite. Plant beans, corn, or other large seeds between the glass and the paper, about one and one-half to two inches down from the top. Water one set of seeds, but not the other. Ask, "What must we give to seeds to make them sprout?"

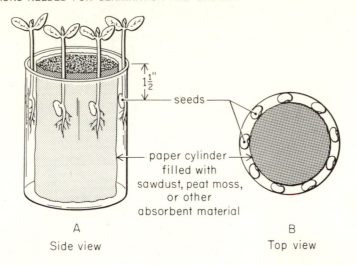

$1\frac{1}{2}''$

— seeds —

paper cylinder —
filled with
sawdust, peat moss,
or other
absorbent material

A
Side view

B
Top view

Plants need water to grow. Plants will die if they do not get water.

Question: Besides good soil, what do plants need to grow well? Set up two plants in a warm, sunny location. Have the children water one plant regularly. Do not give *any* water to the second plant. Let the children observe the changes in the two plants over several weeks. Ask, "Why is this plant dying [the one not given water]?"

Warmth

Seeds need warmth to sprout.

Question: Besides water, what do seeds need to sprout? Place paper cylinders in two tall peanut butter jars. Have the children fill each jar with sawdust, cotton, peat moss, or vermiculite. Plant beans, corn or other large seeds between the glass and the paper about one and one-half to two inches down from the top. Now place one jar in the refrigerator and the other in a warm, dark place. Keep the planting medium in both jars moist but not sopping wet. Ask, "Why don't the seeds in the refrigerator sprout?" Have the children put their hands in the refrigerator to feel how cold it is and in the warm, dark place to feel how warm it is.

Place a piece of window glass (about 8 inches by 12 inches) on the table. Lay strips of wood about one-half inch thick around three sides. Fill the center with soil. About one to one and one-half inches from the top, plant a row of large seeds—beans, corn, etc. Place another piece of glass on top and tie or tape the two pieces of glass together. Set the apparatus upright in a pan of water and put it into the refrigerator. Place a duplicate set in a warm, dark place. Or set up the apparatus, but in place of soil, use cotton batting.

Plants need warmth to grow.

Question: Besides soil and water, what do plants need to grow well? During that part of the winter when there is a heavy frost or snow on the ground, give the children two potted plants—philodendron, geranium, etc. Have the children place one plant outside; the other, in a sunny window in the classroom. Have them give each plant the same amount of water at the same time every day for two or three days. Ask, "Which plant grows better?"

Light

Plants need light to grow. They will not stay green and keep on growing if they do not have light.

Question: Besides water and warmth, what do plants need to grow well? Set up two potted plants of the same kind. Put one in the dark and the other in a warm, sunny spot. Let the children observe the plants for several weeks. Ask, "On which plant are the leaves turning yellow? What does one plant get that the other doesn't?"

Set up duplicate flower pots or milk

cartons. Plant the same kind of seeds in each container. Put one container in a dark location and the other in the light. The seeds in both containers will sprout and grow, but only the plants in the light will be green. The Plants in the dark will turn yellow and die eventually. (This will take several weeks because the seeds have enough food stored in them to keep the plants growing a long time.)

New Plants and Their Development

A. Plants make new plants in different ways

Some plants grow from seeds.

Have the children plant seeds and watch them as they grow into plants.

Trees grow from seeds.

Gather seeds from such trees as maple, oak, buckeye, etc. Let the children plant these seeds and watch them as they develop into young trees. Suspend an avocado seed (using toothpicks to hold it in place) with the blunt end down, in a glass of water. Let the children watch the seed sprout and the young tree develop roots and leaves.

Some plants grow from bulbs.

Have the children plant such bulbs as daffodil, Chinese lily, hyacinth, etc. in trays or dishes containing sand or gravel and water. Encourage them to watch as the bulbs send up shoots and develop blossoms.

Some plants grow from slips or stem cuttings.

Gather branches of willow, poplar, maple, oak, forsythia, etc. Cut the branches into six-inch lengths. In making each cutting, make a slanting cut one-fourth inch above the top bud and one-fourth inch below the lowest bud. Have the children put these cuttings into glasses of water and watch them sprout leaves and roots. The children may plant the rooted cuttings in pots of good soil. Make cuttings of geraniums or some similar plants. Remove all leaves except two at the top. Have the children plant these cuttings in flower pots or boxes containing a mixture of sand and peat moss. The cuttings should be planted with two-thirds of their length in the soil. Keep the sand moist. Place a piece of glass on the top of the box or pot to prevent loss of moisture, or invert a glass jar over each of the cuttings. The formation of roots will be speeded up if the base of each cutting is dipped in a rooting powder (Rootone, etc.).

Some plants grow from leaves. Secure some leaves of gloxinia or African violet. Show the children how to plant the leaves in a box or flower pot by inserting the leaf stalk (petiole) into the soil. Cover the box or flower pot with glass to prevent loss of moisture.

Some plants grow from roots. In the spring, have the children partially submerge sweet potatoes (roots) in jars of water and watch as the shoots develop. Place the jars in a well-lighted window. Let the children plant dahlia roots in boxes of soil or in flower pots filled with good loam. (Each root *must* have a bit of stem attached or it will not grow.)

B. Plants change as they grow—from sprouting seeds to flowers, to fruits, and back again to seeds

Plants grow from seeds to plants, to flowers, to fruits, and back to seeds again. Have the children plant some seeds of quick-growing annual plants and follow the sprouting and subsequent growth of the plants, the development of flowers, and the reproduction of seeds.

Flowers make fruits, and the fruits have seeds in them.

Take the children for a walk around the school grounds and select several plants to watch regularly. Have them observe the plants day after day to see how, after the petals are gone, fruits develop, each containing seeds.

Cut open a number of fruits. Let the children see that each fruit contains one or more seeds.

Seed containers usually open when the seeds are ripe and ready to sprout.

Secure a variety of mature but unopened fruits—yellow pine, Digger pine, beans, peas, etc. Put these unopened fruits on a table. As they dry, they will break open and release their seeds. Let the children plant some of these bean and pea seeds and watch the plants appear and grow.

C. Most plants grow from sprouting seeds

People plant some seeds.

Show pictures of people planting seeds.

Seeds are planted at different depths in the ground. Big seeds are planted deeper than little seeds.

Help the children to plant radish, bean, or corn seeds in a flower pot or box. Focus their attention on the depth at which the different seeds are planted. Radish seeds are barely covered with fine soil; beans and corn are planted about one inch deep.

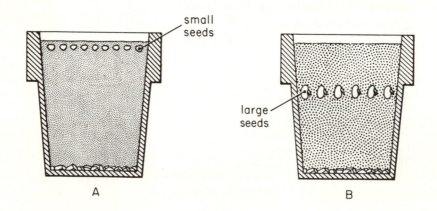

small seeds

large seeds

A   B

Seeds sprout when planted in soil.

Use the previous activity. (Remember always to sterilize flower pots before use. Soak them in a solution of potassium permanganate and scrub with a coarse brush. Most flower pots are contaminated with mold spores.)

Some seeds sprout faster than others.

Let the children place a wet cloth on a dish. Scatter radish, bean, and corn seeds over one-half of the cloth. Fold the other half of the cloth over them. Place a lid on the dish. Have the children observe the seeds each day. The radish seeds will sprout first.

Let the children plant radish seeds in one flower pot or box, bean seeds in another, squash seeds in another, and corn in a fourth. Or plant several of each kind of seeds in a group in different parts of the flower box or pot. Water the seeds regularly. Radish seeds will sprout very rapidly; beans and corn will come up later.

When seeds sprout, roots grow down and leaves grow up.

Place a sheet of blotting paper on a sheet of glass. Wet the blotting paper. Sprinkle a row of radish seeds across the top of the blotting paper one inch down from the top. Place another sheet of glass on top and tie or tape the two pieces of glass together. Set the glass and blotting paper in a pan of water. (Have about an inch of water in the pan.) After the seeds have sprouted and grown for a day, turn the glass at right angles. The children will see that the roots grow down and the shoots grow up, even when the plants are turned on their sides for a time.

When seeds sprout, the baby plants in

Plant some lima beans in a box. Place a very light block of wood over each seed. Let *the seeds push up hard to get out of the ground.*

the children see that the emerging shoots lift the blocks and move them aside.

Plants change in size and shape as they grow, flower, and produce fruit.

Let the children plant bush beans in boxes or flower pots or in a selected spot in the schoolyard. Have them watch the changes the plants undergo in size and shape as they grow, flower, and produce fruit.

EXPLORING, COMPARING, AND SEEING RELATIONSHIPS

A. Flowers attract insects; insects help flowers to make new seeds

The sweet-smelling juice (nectar) and showy petals of flowers attract insects; insects help flowers to make new seeds.

Question: What kind of flowers do honey bees (and other insects) visit when they gather nectar? In the spring, take the children out of doors to watch bees flying from flower to flower. Show them the heads of grasses. You will have to tell them that the heads of grasses are flowers. Ask, "Do honey bees visit the grasses? Then what kinds of flowers do they visit?" Help them to understand that bees go to flowers that are shallow, have colored petals, and a sweet fragrance. Ask, "How are the flowers that insects visit different from the grass flowers?" Tell them that bees do not take nectar from honeysuckles because the flowers are too deep for the honey bees to get to the nectar.

B. Fruits have seeds to help them make new plants

Fruits have seeds inside them.

Question: What is a fruit? Place a variety of fruits on the table, including a bell pepper and tomato. Cut the fruits open. Ask, "In what way are all these fruits the same?" Help the children to conclude that all fruits have seeds inside them. (This is the definition of a fruit insofar as little children can comprehend it.)

C. Some seeds are planted deeper in the ground than others

Big seeds are planted deeper than small seeds.

Question: Do we plant all seeds at the same depth in the ground? Why? Let the children plant seeds in pairs of boxes or flower pots. In one box or pot, have them plant bean seeds one inch deep. Then plant radish seeds, barely covering them with soil. In the other box or flower pot, have them plant the radish seeds two inches deep and barely cover the bean seeds with soil. (Smaller seeds are even more satisfactory. The small seeds should be planted so that few, if any, can push through the surface of the soil.) Ask, "Why do we plant small seeds close to the surface of the soil?" Place a cylinder of paper toweling or blotting paper inside each of two tall empty peanut butter jars. Fill the centers of the jars with sawdust, cotton, etc. and press down firmly. Plant the two jars with radish and bean seeds. In one jar, place the bean seeds close to the top between the glass and the cylinder. Plant radish seeds an inch or an inch and one-half down from the top, also between the glass and the cylinder. Reverse the depths of the seeds in the second jar. Focus the children's attention on the difficulty the radish seeds have in making their way to the surface when they have been planted so deep.